The Family That Conquered Everest

by Alan Mallory

RMB

RMB | Rocky Mountain Books Ltd.
rmbooks.com
@rmbooks
facebook.com/rmbooks

Cataloguing data available from Library and Archives Canada
ISBN 978-1-77160-130-6 (paperback)
ISBN 978-1-77160-131-3 (electronic)

Cover photo: Zzvet (iStock)

Printed and bound in Canada by Friesens

Distributed in Canada by Heritage Group Distribution
and in the U.S. by Publishers Group West

For information on purchasing bulk quantities of this book, or to
obtain media excerpts or invite the author to speak at an event,
please visit rmbooks.com and select the "Contact Us" tab.

We acknowledge the financial support of the Government of Canada through the Canada
Book Fund and the Canada Council for the Arts, and of the province of British Columbia
through the British Columbia Arts Council and the Book Publishing Tax Credit.

This book is dedicated to my grandfather, Wilbert Eugene Mallory, who passed away in 2011. I am thankful for all the life lessons and practical knowledge he passed on to me that helped nurture and craft the person that I am today.

Table of Contents

Acknowledgements

THERE ARE MANY PEOPLE THAT I WOULD LIKE TO acknowledge thank for their contributions to this book, their participation in the anecdotes contained within it and their influence in the exciting and interesting journey that my life has been thus far. I am fortunate to have so many wonderful people in my life.

First, I would like to thank my family for their love and support, especially my parents for raising me the way they did and for all the fabulous adventures I have been honoured to take part in. To my brother and sister, Adam and Laura, you have been the best siblings I could ever ask for, and I look forward to many more years of excitement and camaraderie in our future ventures.

Many of my friends and co-workers have been kind enough to read through and comment on the draft versions of this book, and for that I am very grateful as well. Your feedback and support have been invaluable throughout the process, so thank you for devoting your time.

Most important, I would like to thank my beautiful wife, Natalie, who loves me for who I am and has stuck with me through all of the crazy ideas I have conjured up and ventures I have commenced during our marriage thus far. Thank you for your encouragement and trust. It is a great privilege and a blessing for me to have such a wonderful partner in life to love and to share the journey with.

1

My Family

I WAS CLINGING TO THE JAGGED, EXPOSED ROCK ON THE summit ridge of Mount Everest, and the last of my oxygen cylinders had been depleted. I had just collapsed on the icy, cold surface beneath me, and I frantically tore off my now useless oxygen mask, gasping desperately for sufficient air to satisfy my starving lungs. My inner core was filled with a strange, bitter-cold sensation, and my limbs were trembling violently out of my control. My mind raced, and although I fought hard against the building fright within me, I began to panic. I still remember that terrible feeling, and the memory brings back a chill even to this day.

My thoughts were drawn to the nearly 200 other climbers who had lost their lives on Everest, and I couldn't help but realize that the state I was entering into was exactly the condition that would have befallen many of those climbers shortly before they lost their lives. Many other thoughts and feelings flashed through my mind and body during that dreadful period as well — sadness, helplessness, confusion, and even some feelings of regret — but all of these were dwarfed by the solemn realization that was becoming more and more of a reality: "I am going to die on this mountain."

Everyone has dreams of one sort or another in life

— aspirations of becoming someone important or doing something significant with their time here on earth. It is only human nature for us to have these dreams. Even in early childhood, each of us begins setting lofty goals for the type of person we want to be and what we want to do with our lives. Unfortunately, some of these dreams can get lost in the hectic busyness of our daily lives. It is important to dream, though. It gives us motivation and something to look forward to, something to set our sights on.

This book is about my family and how we set and collectively achieved one of our common dreams: to climb to the highest point on earth, the summit of Mount Everest. I was encouraged to share this story by the many individuals, and especially the families, who found our journey inspirational and personally moving. Close-knit families are becoming a rarity nowadays, and the strong camaraderie my family shares is a great gift and a privilege.

I am the middle child of a unique family of five from a little village in Southern Ontario by the name of Utopia. Although many would argue that it is not quite the "ideally perfect place" the name suggests, it is a quiet, rural area off the beaten track and has several wilderness areas nearby. I expect this is the reason my parents chose this area in which to live and raise a family.

My upbringing, and that of my brother and sister, was a little different than most, I suppose. We never had a television growing up, and even through our university years the only television my parents had in the house was an old cathode-ray tube that sat in the basement and was rarely used.

Not having a television changed the way we had to entertain ourselves as children. When most of our friends were watching cartoons and their favourite shows, we were obliged to amuse ourselves by exploring the surrounding area and finding other things to do, usually in the outdoors. We didn't have many of the fancy toys that most children have nowadays, either. I guess my mother and father thought that these playthings were a waste of money, or maybe we couldn't afford them, but for whatever reason, we grew up playing with wooden blocks and homemade games instead of trendy brand-name toys.

What we did do, though, was spend a lot of time exploring and taking part in various outdoor activities with our parents. Mom would spend all summer with us up at the cottage, and for as long as I can remember, we have been going on hikes and camping trips as a family.

My father planted the competitive seed in us at a very early age. I can recall his entering us in mountain bike races, running competitions, and triathlons shortly after I learned to ride a bike. I didn't always enjoy all of these outdoor activities, but eventually the competitive spark and sense of adventure began to grow inside of me, as it did in my brother and sister, and we have retained it ever since.

We definitely have our father to thank for this strong sense of adventure and also for pointing us in the right direction when it came to setting and following through with our goals. Dad has always been a goal-setter, and he doesn't let much come in the way of achieving his goals once they have been set. Although this focused perseverance is frustrating for my mother at times, it is a quality I much admire and hope to be able to instil in my own children.

My father is competitive in all aspects of life. He has always enjoyed individual sports and racing where he could push his own body and mind to the next level.

Dad is a general insurance broker by trade, and he owns his own small brokerage. Although owning a business resulted in his having to spend many late nights at the office, it also gave him flexibility in his working hours and the opportunity to take time off when he wanted. This allowed him to create and maintain a good balance between work and his numerous outdoor leisure activities.

Never liking a dull moment, Dad is always trying to avoid sitting around and doing nothing by planning ahead to make sure that every valuable moment in life is well spent.

My mother is the caregiver of the family. She is the glue that holds our family together, and she deals with the many issues and crises that arise from time to time. She was the one who would wake up at all hours of the night to take us to the hospital or to look after us while we were sick. Mom has a very bubbly and kind personality and an unmistakable laugh that can be recognized from a surprisingly long way away.

Although my mother did not grow up in an adventuresome household, after meeting my father she adopted the outdoor lifestyle and has enjoyed it ever since. She loves the tranquility of the outdoors and spends a lot of her free time canoeing, snow-shoeing, cross-country skiing, and enjoying other quiet outdoor activities that allow her to appreciate the fresh air.

Although Mom doesn't have quite the love for climbing and the arguably risky endeavours that my father does, she has been on her fair share of high mountains and been stuck in more challenging and hair-raising situations than I'm sure she cares to remember.

My older brother, Adam, is the "tinkerer" and the "fixer" of the family. His inquisitive mind always needs to know how everything works, and for his whole life, he has been taking things apart to discover their inner workings and then trying to put them back together. I can remember the first few remote-control cars that he was given. Adam took them apart and often forgot how to put them back together or lost some of the pieces. He ended with a few ruined remote-control vehicles, but he learned a lot in the process and has been able to repair many broken-down electronic gadgets ever since.

I am very close with Adam and can say that we truly enjoy spending time together. We both have creative minds, and we have invented and constructed many different contraptions together over the years. We are extremely competitive with each other, and if one of us does something daring or crazy, then the other will have to try to match or outdo him. Adam also does a lot of reading and research into how things work, and he knows a little bit about everything. Like the rest of us, Adam loves adventure and would prefer being outdoors exploring over anything else.

My younger sister, Laura, is the social butterfly of the family. She loves to hang out with her friends, party, and chat for hours on the telephone. She is no slouch, though, and has always managed to keep up with the rest of us in our competitive endeavours. I have to say she has an amazing inner strength and determination that enables her to keep pace with her older brothers, and we usually don't make it easy! Laura is very strong willed and is not afraid of a challenge.

As for myself, I guess you could say that I am the academic of the family. I never had any trouble in school and didn't seem to have to work as hard as everyone else. I wouldn't say that I am especially intelligent; I just consistently learned how to recognize and manage systems to my own advantage.

I have always enjoyed problem-solving and coming up with new ideas. Once I start thinking of a problem or a new idea, I find myself continuing to think about it until I have figured it out. This can be quite frustrating at times; I often find it difficult to fall asleep if my mind is churning, but I do get a sense of accomplishment when I eventually resolve the problem.

For leisure activities, I enjoy anything that triggers an adrenaline rush. My favourites are skiing and white water kayaking. Both of these sports are fast-paced and make me feel elated and free.

Many people find the adventuresome lifestyle that my family leads strange or stressful, but it is what seems natural to us. We are very fortunate that we have all learned to enjoy similar activities and challenges because it means spending time together is not a struggle but a privilege, and it helps ensure that our family get-togethers and outings are always an adventure.

Throughout this book, I will refer back to aspects of my family and upbringing to provide a background picture of the habits and activities (as well as the mental and physical preparations) that I believe allowed us to be successful. One of the common questions that my family has been asked is, when most families cannot even get along around the dinner table without problems, how were we able to survive on Mount Everest together in such horrible conditions for such a long period of time?

The answer, I think, is by conditioning ourselves, mostly mentally, to maintain focus on the end goal and to do whatever it takes to make it a reality. I believe it is a lifestyle choice, mostly made by my parents during our childhoods, which helped us with this conditioning and prepared us to take on this incredible challenge.

This isn't to say that the way we live or the things we did as a family are the only secrets to family success, but I do think that lifestyle choices, determining what we give our time to, and the effort we put into doing things as a family are major contributors to this type of mental conditioning.

To be successful in any difficult endeavour, a team needs to ensure that there is a level of respect and trust between team members. Many teams fall apart from lack of these two crucial elements. They can be difficult to develop and even more difficult to sustain at times, but they are essential to the success of a team.

The anecdotes and reflections that I share at different points throughout this book are to illustrate some of the ways we developed respect and trust for each other. I believe that this was the biggest advantage we had over many other teams, and it was without a doubt the most significant contributor to our success.

2

Our Collective Dream

THE IDEA OF ATTEMPTING TO CLIMB TO THE HIGHEST POINT on earth began with my father. Although Dad had been active in hiking and exploring his whole life, he didn't actually start doing any serious climbing until he was about thirty-five.

His first real climb was during a vacation with my mother in Mérida, Venezuela. He wanted to do some hiking in the area, and the local hiking trail was closed, so Dad started talking to some young university students about where else they might be allowed to hike. One of the students said that his brother, Neduy, could guide them on a hike in the mountains, which sounded pretty interesting to my father, so they agreed to meet Neduy at daybreak the next morning. Much to their surprise, Neduy showed up with climbing harnesses, ropes, ice axes, and crampons. They were expecting to do some moderate hiking, and suddenly their "hike" took on a whole new meaning. They were beginning to think that it might be more than they were prepared for.

Nevertheless, they stuck with the plan and took a gondola about seven kilometres up the mountain to the starting point of the climb. After getting off the gondola, Neduy started by stepping over a safety rope with a sign that read "*Peligro*," meaning "danger" in Spanish, and the first descent turned out to be down a sheer cliff, where Neduy kept telling my mother, in Spanish, "Trust in me and in God." My father kept looking over at Mom, ready for her to suggest turning back at any moment, but she never did.

Although Dad got serious mountain sickness, an altitude-related condition resulting in severe headaches and nausea from the high elevation, and they had to stop and spend the night in a *refugio* high up in the mountains because he was too sick to continue, it was a spectacular climb; and after that, I guess Dad was hooked.

Several years later, after having the three of us children, Mom and Dad decided to take a trip to Africa with the plan to climb Mount Kilimanjaro in Tanzania, the highest mountain on the continent at 19,341 feet (5,895 metres) in elevation. It is not a particularly technical mountain to climb, but Dad again had a lot of trouble with altitude sickness when they neared the summit.

They didn't do any more high-altitude climbing for years after that, but when my brother Adam was nineteen, Dad decided it would be a good adventure for him and Adam to attempt to climb the highest mountain in South America — Mount Aconcagua in Argentina.

Mount Aconcagua is again not so technical a climb because it is a dormant volcano; but it is the highest mountain in the world outside of the Himalayan mountain range, reaching 22,841 feet (6,962 metres) at its peak.

It was a demanding climb because of the serious elevation gain and had its fair share of difficulties, including having to wade across a rushing glacial-melt river that nearly swept both of them off their feet and down one of the mountain's rocky slopes. They did, however, make it to the summit, and although it was very painful at times, especially for Adam, it gave them a real sense of confidence and accomplishment.

These summit successes started to create more and more

passion for my father about mountain climbing, and got him thinking very seriously about some of the other mountains in the world and what other challenging peaks he could attempt.

Only a few years later, when I turned nineteen as well, Dad asked me if I wanted to attempt to climb the highest mountain in North America, Denali (also called Mount McKinley), with him. I agreed, and at the end of my second year of university, we flew to Anchorage, Alaska, to make the attempt. Denali, at 20,320 feet (6,194 metres), is a very technical and cold mountain, and we encountered an array of frightening and dangerous situations while we were there. We did success-fully summit after almost two weeks of climbing, and it was an extraordinary experience, especially for me, as it was my first high-altitude endeavour. The vast array of mountain peaks and magnificent glaciers that we witnessed from the summit was truly incredible.

After this success on Denali, Dad began to develop the goal for himself of reaching the top of each one of what are known as the Seven Summits, the highest mountains on each of the seven continents. Having two of the more difficult mountains already conquered, Dad decided he would continue climbing and see if it were possible. He wanted to be the first person in the world to climb each of the Seven Summits with at least one member of his immediate family.

Dad and Mom climbed Mount Kosciuszko, the highest in Australia, in 2005. It takes only a day to climb but is one of the seven, so Dad needed to check it off the list. It gave them an excuse to visit Australia as well, which they thoroughly enjoyed.

When my sister, Laura, was nineteen, she and Dad flew to Russia to climb Mount Elbrus, the highest mountain in Europe. Of the numerous challenges they encountered on Elbrus, the most notable was a fierce lightning storm that was so intense and close by that the electrical charge made all the hairs on their bodies stand up on end and the electrically charged air actually generated a buzzing noise. They had to lie down on the ground and wait out the storm before continuing on.

On the way back from Russia, they flew to Africa, where they met my mother, and stopped by Tanzania to climb Mount Kilimanjaro, the second ascent of Kilimanjaro for my father and mother. There are two peaks on the rim of Kilimanjaro, which is a volcanic caldera, one slightly higher than the other; they had climbed to the lower of the two peaks the first time they were there, so my father decided he had to climb it again, climbing to the highest point, of course, to make it official.

It was around that time when we had our first discussion about Mount Everest. We were sitting around the dinner table one evening, and Dad unexpectedly asked if anyone would be interested in attempting to climb it. We hadn't given it much thought before that, at least I hadn't, but we all said that that sounded like a pretty good idea.

That is how it started. It was a very short conversation, but it sparked our interest and planted the seed of an undeniable challenge and a feeling of excitement that continued to grow over time.

In the years following that brief conversation, each of us started thinking more and more about the challenge. After I did a bit of research on the mountain and developed an understanding of the difficulties involved, it became evident that I was drawn to the undertaking somehow, and reaching the summit became a personal goal for myself, as it did for the rest of my family.

Although we started thinking about the challenge a few years before we actually attempted it, the majority of the logistics didn't come together until a few months before we set out. This was largely unavoidable.

Firstly, Adam and Laura were still in university, and the climb was during exam season. They had to wait until the beginning of their semesters to ask their professors for special consideration and permission to move their exam dates or risk losing the semester. As well, I had just started working for a large engineering firm and I had to go to my superiors and ask for a two and a half month "holiday" after having worked for them for only a short time. Needless to say, the response to this request could have gone a couple of different ways, but fortunately they were very supportive of the expedition.

The last two months prior to our flight departures were extremely hectic. There were hundreds of emails back and forth, between family members and between us and the outfitter that we had decided to use and our many equipment suppliers.

There is an enormous amount of very expensive, specialized gear required for a climb of such magnitude, and a lot of the specialized equipment could not be found in Canada, so it had to be ordered from other countries. Dad actually had to take a flight down to a little village in Ohio called Granville, which was the only place where he was able to find and buy our high-altitude mountaineering boots.

We tried to get sponsorship for the expedition to offset the high costs, but it was a difficult thing to do with the short lead time we had. Overall, we were able to raise only enough money to cover about 15 percent of the costs. It is not uncommon for a person to spend over US$100,000 on an Everest attempt, and many people do, each and every year. We tried to arrange the expedition as economically as we could without sacrificing any of the important safety equipment, but the expedition still ended up costing us about US$45,000 per person.

There was so much organizing, preparing, and packing to do in the last few weeks before we left that our departure date seemed to speed toward us like an out-of-control train. And before we knew it, the day was upon us.

3

The Approach

ON APRIL 5, 2008, DAD, LAURA, AND I WOKE EARLY TO FINISH packing the last of our equipment and belongings. Natalie, my girlfriend at the time, who is now my wife, was with us in the morning to say her final goodbyes. Natalie had also offered to drive us to the airport in Toronto. We had spent the last few months mentally, physically, and logistically preparing for this daunting attempt of Mount Everest, and it was finally time to embark.

I had been watching our departure date approach with mixed feelings. A part of me felt the before-stage excitement and anticipation for the great adventure that we had ahead of us, but there was also an element of trepidation within me, fear of the dangers ahead of us, and concern that something bad would happen to one or more of us.

Natalie and I had also both been dreading having to say goodbye to each other. We had become very close and were not looking forward to being without any reliable means of communication for the nearly two and a half months that my family and I were expected to be climbing to reach the top and return — what seemed like nearly a lifetime for both of us.

The emotional mixture was different from the feeling at the beginning of a normal trip or vacation because there was that black thought in the back of my mind that some climbers never come back from Mount Everest. I knew these negative thoughts were detrimental, and I tried to suppress them whenever I could, but like a cork on water, they kept coming to the surface.

With the huge amount of equipment we had been procuring and organizing for a year, our home looked like a sporting goods store, with mountains of gear throughout the house.

Although we had a lot of high-quality equipment from past climbs, much of it was not adequate for the harsh conditions and cold temperatures unique to the high Himalayan mountain range that we would be encountering as we climbed Mount Everest.

For example, in the past, we had used large mountaineering boots with warm liners and insoles protected by a durable plastic shell, known as a "double mountaineering boot." These had worked exceptionally well and taken us to the top of many high mountains. However, because of the extremely low air pressure and oxygen availability at the high elevation of Everest, blood circulation is very poor and heat loss from your extremities must be virtually eliminated to avoid losing your toes and fingers to frostbite.

There is often no place nearby to gain shelter to warm up before you lose sensation in your toes and fingers. Many climbers have faced amputation from being ill-prepared for the frigid conditions, and for this reason we all required special one-piece boots with protection up to our knees, designed to be used on the 8,000-plus-metre mountains of the world, found only in the Himalayas of Southern Asia.

The high-altitude specialized mitts and parkas that we had ordered were also the warmest we could find, filled with goose down and other high-calibre insulating materials designed to stand up to the toughest conditions. We didn't want to take any additional risks from having inadequate gear, and by the time we had finished packing, we felt very well-equipped for the challenge ahead.

My mother had flown over on March 27, earlier than the rest of us, for a few different reasons. To augment her fitness and climbing experience before our arrival, Mom wanted to do a climb to the Tibetan Base Camp and then meet up with the rest of us on the south side. Mount Everest can be climbed from the north side, through Tibet, or from the south side, through the country of Nepal, which was our chosen route. She wanted some extra time to acclimatize and condition herself, and her early arrival would help accomplish this.

Adam was also not with us as we drove to the airport. Being in his last year of university, he had to write a few exams, which delayed his departure by about a week. Our plan was to meet him partway along the trek in to Base Camp.

Because of our later start, most climbers had already arrived and had begun their climb. We were about two weeks behind and could only hope that our fitness levels would allow us to make up time before the summer monsoon weather would drive us off the mountain.

At the airport, each of us grabbed two or three of our heavy canvas bags, which were colour-coordinated for each person, and awkwardly made our way into the airport, half-carrying and half-dragging our mountain of luggage. We were well over the permissible weight that the airline allowed on an international flight. However, we managed to get everything checked in without paying any extra fees through some smooth talking and by explaining the challenge we were about to undertake to the gentleman behind the counter.

In front of the security gates was where I had to say my final goodbyes to Natalie. I remember feeling very emotional and torn over my decision to leave as I watched her eyes filling up with tears as she first hugged Laura and then embraced me one final time. It must have been hard for her, knowing the risks we would face where we were heading. I stayed to watch her leave and then turned to pass through the final security gate and catch up with my father and sister.

It was an extremely long flight, which took us over the top of the globe, hugging the North Pole before heading south toward China. We were seated at the very back of the plane, and our seats hardly reclined at all because there was a wall directly behind us, so our training for discomfort started right at the beginning of the trip.

Fortunately, there were a few decent movies to pass the time and distract us from any negative thoughts that might have surfaced. After more than fifteen hours of flying, we finally landed in Hong Kong for a four-hour layover. I tried to get a bit of sleep on the hard benches in the Hong Kong airport but didn't really get much due to the constant movement around us and the loud Chinese messages which blared over the loudspeakers every few minutes. Eventually, we boarded a much smaller aircraft which took us on a five-hour flight to Kathmandu, the bustling capital city of Nepal.

Kathmandu, as with most of Nepal, is extremely poor and densely populated. It is the largest city in Nepal and relies heavily on tourism to support its fragile economy. Hinduism and Buddhism are the two prominent religions and the city has a unique cultural and architectural heritage with a lot of old buildings and historical monuments, the oldest of which date back nearly two thousand years.

When we arrived in Kathmandu, we were all very tired, and all we wanted to do was find a place to sleep. After collecting our luggage in the airport, we were met by three representatives from the outfitting company Summit Climb, which we were using to supply us with food, support, and other services for the climb. They helped us carry our heavy bags and loaded them into a van. We all clambered into the van after them, and before long, we were swerving down the narrow Kathmandu streets.

Even though the van was fairly small, we had difficulty

making some of the tight turns along the way. We saw many small climbing shops and a lot of interesting buildings as we bumped along, and we were relieved when we finally arrived at our destination — a small hotel called the Hotel Beijing.

Although the hotel would be considered very basic by North American standards, it was slightly larger and cleaner than the rundown buildings we had seen along the way, and the room rates were quite inexpensive. Laura took her own room, and Dad and I decided to share a room.

There were no elevators in the Hotel Beijing, which we later learned is due to the rolling electricity blackouts that the city experiences every day. Because of this, we took turns carrying our heavy canvas bags up the large staircase to the third floor.

Our room was simple, with a partially shuttered window looking across a narrow street at a brick wall. The mattresses were filled with straw or a type of grass by the look and feel of them, but we were thankful to have a place to lay our heads.

By that time it was midnight local time, but we were not sleepy because of the twelve-hour time difference between Canada and Nepal, so the three of us decided to go out in front of the hotel for a short stroll to check out our surroundings.

The tiny shops adjacent to and across from the hotel entrance had long since been closed and barred shut for the night, and the narrow streets were completely deserted. We didn't go very far before we returned to our rooms. We knew we needed to sleep, so we lay in bed and eventually dozed off, getting a few hours of shut-eye.

We woke up early the next morning, partly because of jet lag and also because of the noise of the city awakening. Kathmandu was a completely different city in the daytime.

I walked out onto a small balcony section of the hallway by our room and was greeted by the sight of a city come to life. The street in front of the hotel was crowded with a frenzy of pedestrians, motorcycles, small cars, and peddlers. I could detect right away that the air quality was very poor, with a pungent odour of dust and garbage. The air felt thick and uncomfortable to my lungs. In exhaustion, I made a joke that the city should be called "Crapmandu," and although in hindsight I understand this was inappropriate, the name stuck for the entire trip.

Dan Mazur, the head of our outfitting organization, was also staying in the Beijing Hotel, on the second floor, which was the main reason we chose to stay there — so it would be easy to connect with him. There was a small Summit Climb office attached to the hotel, and we thought it would be very convenient to be as close as possible to the office for logistical reasons.

We had arranged to meet and have breakfast with Dan Mazur, so we made our way down to the lobby and out into the courtyard. Dan was waiting for us, and we shook hands.

I was glad to finally meet the man with whom we had been conversing via email for many months. He was a tall and cheery man. Although I knew he had done a great deal of climbing, I must admit he didn't look much like a mountain climber at first glance because he was limping around on crutches when we first met him. He had been in a bicycling accident prior to arriving in Nepal and had broken his leg quite badly.

Dan flagged down a taxi and negotiated a price with the driver in broken Nepalese. We all crammed into the tiny taxi, which appeared to be ready to fall apart at any moment, and before we knew it we were bouncing and swerving down the tiny streets once again.

The traffic laws in Kathmandu are nonexistent or unenforced, and the drivers all love to use their horns very frequently, so they are almost constantly honking at someone or something. There was gridlocked traffic in many places throughout the city. It was almost comical watching the vehicles inch their way closer to intersections until nobody could move at all.

After about fifteen minutes, we arrived at our destination, a small restaurant with a sign reading *Mike's Breakfast*. The waiter who greeted us, and who may have been Mike himself, led us outside into the courtyard, and we sat ourselves around one of the small tables.

I had a lot of questions for Dan Mazur during our hearty breakfast of local meats, eggs and porridge, especially about the current political situation between Nepal and China and whether or not this would prevent us from climbing. The Olympics were set to take place in Beijing that summer, and the Chinese wanted to bring the Olympic torch to the top of Everest as part of the torch run.

About a month before the climbing season was to begin, the Chinese government declared that they were closing the Tibetan side of Mount Everest to climbers. They did this so that there would not be other climbers getting in the way of their Olympic torch team and, more important, so that they would not receive any negative publicity from demonstrating Tibetans or others who believed that Tibet should be freed from Chinese rule. The Chinese have occupied Tibet since they invaded the country in 1950, and the Tibetan people saw the Olympics as a great way to get worldwide attention on the issue of regaining their independence.

Since we were planning on climbing on the Nepalese side of the mountain, we were not immediately affected by the initial announcement of closing the Tibetan side. However, the Chinese were providing financial support to Nepal, one of the poorest countries in the world, and as a result they had a great deal of influence there.

The Chinese persuaded the Nepalese government to put strict controls and restrictions on the Nepalese side of the mountain as well: Nepalese military personnel were sent up to Everest Base Camp to search people's gear bags for flags and other propaganda relating to the freeing of Tibet.

They also were instructed to prevent anyone from climbing too high on the mountain until the Chinese Olympic torch team had reached the summit, at which point the Chinese government would give the Nepalese army permission to remove the restrictions. They were afraid that climbers from the Nepalese south side would climb up and over to the north side and interfere with the climb, a somewhat inconceivable likelihood.

Unfortunately, Dan Mazur did not know much more than we did about the events on the mountain, but he did not seem concerned about the strict climbing restrictions. I was still quite concerned and did not like the prospect of starting a climb that we might be forced to abandon, but there was nothing we could do.

Once we had finished our breakfast, we headed back to the hotel, and Dan took us up the steep, narrow steps that led to the Summit Climb office.

Inside the office we met Mauri, one of Dan's local employees who dealt with the books, money, and other background tasks. There were many pictures and posters on the walls recording previous clients' ascents of Everest, and it was a comfortable area to discuss logistics.

We talked a lot about the route into Base Camp and what we could expect. Dan warned us about the dry air and dust that can be encountered in the Khumbu Valley, which leads into Base Camp. He also warned us about all the illnesses that are difficult to avoid during the climb. We were being very careful not to pick up any bugs in Kathmandu, trying to wear handkerchiefs over our mouths when we were out walking around.

We needed to purchase some equipment that we hadn't had room to bring over from Canada, so Dan sent Deha, Mauri's younger brother, with us into the streets of Kathmandu to buy supplies.

Wow! What an experience, just walking down the narrow,

dusty streets and seeing how the people live. There were people scurrying about like ants on a disturbed anthill and more and more gridlocked traffic at every intersection, with the constant clamour of drivers blowing their horns every chance they could. The streets were extremely crowded with pedestrians, and many motorcycles darted among them as though oblivious to their presence. We had to really watch that we did not get clipped by a vehicle, because there wasn't much room to get out of the way and the drivers didn't seem to care.

There were no big department stores that we could find in Kathmandu. Instead, it seemed that everyone owned a tiny, open-concept store, selling the same wares as everyone else. Peddlers and beggars on the street were constantly following us and reciting their sales pitches over and over. They continued to follow us until Deha told them to leave us alone — and even then, some would persist.

I did quite enjoy bargaining in the local shops, and I found out quickly that almost everything that is made locally or is not a brand name could be bought for a fraction of the asking price. The frantic peddling of wares, shouting to attract customers, and selling of everything they could was a whole different experience from a western city. I couldn't help but feel sorry for the people, though. They live in that rat race all their lives.

We went to several small climbing shops and bought down-filled pants, sleeping mats, and other equipment. We were warned not to bring inflatable sleeping mats because they always eventually get punctured once on the mountain. Instead, we bought three or four foam-type sleeping mats each, and I bought an inexpensive ice axe as well.

Powerful medications for which you would need a prescription in Canada and most other countries can be bought quite cheaply over the counter at small boutiques in Kathmandu. We bought many of the drugs Dan had suggested. As the medical drugs are so easy to get, they are often not used properly, and thus a good many of the common parasites and bacteria have become immune to typical drugs like ciprofloxacin. One has to use very strong doses to kill the so-called "superbugs" that are fairly prevalent on the mountain and that we would fully experience in the weeks ahead.

The Nepalese people were coming up to an election on April 10, so all of the activists were out on the streets in full force. There were political supporters driving around with megaphones attached to cars and large flags on motorcycles.

Long lines of supporters would go by, shouting slogans and waving their party flags. There was unrest and uncertainty about the election, and we learned that all the roads would be closed to vehicles on Election Day. This happened to be the same day that Adam was going to be arriving in Kathmandu, so we were not sure how Adam would get from the airport to the hotel.

We walked a long way, and my feet were sore by the end of the day. I hadn't been doing much walking in Canada because I had been plagued for quite some time with patellofemoral pain syndrome, and I was trying to let it heal before we left. Patellofemoral pain syndrome is a condition caused by improper tracking of the kneecap, and it is extremely painful. I had been doing exercises to correct the problem, and it was slightly better than it had been in the previous weeks, but I hadn't been able to do any hiking. It had gotten so bad before starting the exercises that I could hardly go up a set of stairs and, naturally, I was having some serious concerns about my ability to climb.

My legs felt like jelly by the time we got back to the hotel. The Achilles tendon in my left heel also was hurting a fair bit, a problem I have had since I partially tore both of my Achilles tendons while climbing Denali in 2004. A dark cloud of doubt was weighing heavily on my mind, and I felt somewhat depressed that there was the very real possibility that my knees and tendons might prevent me from even making it to Base Camp, let alone attempting the summit.

For dinner, we went out with Dan Mazur to a place that was well known for its pizza, so that is what we ordered. Dan warned us about eating foods that we would normally keep refrigerated in Canada. Because of the constant power outages in Kathmandu, it is difficult for them to keep perishables continuously refrigerated, so contracting a food-borne illness was a concern. The pizza was quite good, although everything had a different taste from what we were used to.

Rather than taking a taxi home, we took two rickshaws, which are large tricycles with a two-seat carriage on the back for tourists. Many appear to be held together by good fortune, ready to fall apart at any moment. Just as we were seated and getting ready to leave, a young man who had been looking at us in an odd way reached up to the carriage and tried to steal our camera out of Laura's hand. He would likely have been successful had she not had it tied around her wrist. It was a bit of a scary moment for her, and we watched more carefully for this type of petty theft from that point on. On the narrow, dark streets leading back to the hotel, the guy who was pedalling had to keep jumping off to push the rickshaw out of the potholes. It was quite an experience, far removed from our life back home.

That night, we packed all our gear so that we would be ready for an early departure in the morning. We had tentatively arranged for our flight out of Kathmandu, and we were really hoping that it would not be cancelled due to weather.

Our minds were still alive with all the new sights and sounds of the day, and as night fell, we desperately tried to get some sleep.

4
Taking the First Step

WE WOKE UP EARLY, AT AROUND 4:00 A.M., AFTER GETTING very little sleep. Dan Mazur introduced us to Shera, who would be accompanying us until we arrived at Everest Base Camp. Shera was a short, quiet man, one of the Sherpas who worked for Summit Climb. Sherpas are an important ethnic group in Nepal, and they are the bloodline of people who have been helping climbers at high altitudes in the Himalayas since the beginning of Himalayan mountaineering.

All of the Sherpas are named after one of the days of the week, according to the day they were born, although they usually have a secondary name as well to distinguish them from the many other Sherpas with the same name. They all share the common last name of Sherpa.

Shera did not speak a lot of English and did not speak to us much at all while we were bringing all of our bags down to the lobby and loading them into the Summit Climb van. Dad was frantically rushing around in his usual last-minute fashion, and we decided to leave a few bags containing jeans and other things that we would not be needing on the expedition. We said our goodbyes to Dan and then climbed into the van to depart for the airport.

We sped down the poorly paved and dirt streets, narrowly

missing pedestrians and vehicles along the way. The streets were not as crowded as the day before because it was still quite early in the morning, but there were still plenty of people around.

One interesting fact about Nepal is that, because of the Hindu influence, the cows are sacred and cannot be killed or harmed. They roam freely around the city and take naps wherever they want, often on the pavement or in the middle of the roads, where it is nice and warm. This means that all the vehicles have to swerve around them, and nobody dares to try to move them. They are usually sprawled out and sunning themselves, oblivious to the fact that they are blocking full lanes of traffic and causing dozens of cars to alter their routes.

The airport opened at 6:00 a.m., but we were there an hour early to make sure we got a place on one of the planes headed for Lukla, the small village that acts as the starting point for anyone climbing on or around the Nepalese side of Mount Everest. We put our bags outside of the glass front doors of the airport and waited. As we waited, more and more people began to arrive, some tourists but many locals, until the walkway in front of the doors was completely packed with people.

At around 6:00 a.m., they started to open the front doors, and almost instantaneously there was a stampede of people trying to push their way inside the terminal. What a sight!

The guard at the front doors tried to organize the flow of people into the airport lobby but to no avail. Like a wartime attack, the onslaught of people flooded the doors, and there was no stopping most of them. I found it a bit humorous to watch.

The guard appeared to be trying to stop as many local Nepalese people as possible, but as he was deterring one person, two or three were sneaking under his outstretched arms and into the terminal. Shera stayed outside and passed the bags to me, most of them over the guard's head or under his barricading arms, which were now spread across the doorway. With considerable effort, we finally managed to get all of the bags inside the doors.

The security system at the Kathmandu airport was almost laughable. They had an old-fashioned X-ray baggage scanner near the front doors that all of the bags were supposed to go through. I'm sure that most people didn't bother following this protocol, and I could hardly blame them. The X-ray machine was completely useless because nobody was watching the screen anyway. I think they just had it there to pretend to comply with international security standards; the screen was probably not even plugged in. As well, everyone was forcing their bags through the machine as fast as humanly possible, and there was no way that anything scanned could be identified.

The check-in process was different from anything we were used to as well. We basically just flashed our boarding passes, and they started grabbing our bags and heading off in different directions with them. I half-expected our bags to end up in Australia or Timbuktu because of all the disorganization, but by that time it was too late to do anything about it.

After that, we made our way through a security screening booth where the attendant verbally confirmed that we were not carrying any weapons or prohibited items, and then we went out onto the tarmac, where some buses waited.

The small aircraft used for ferrying people to and from Lukla were lined up on the tarmac as our bus arrived. It looked like something out of an old World War II movie. We watched them all starting and revving their engines until black smoke poured out from every direction. Our airline company, Yeti Airlines, used old, Canadian-made Twin Otter aircraft, painted green. We had no idea where our luggage had gone, but we got off the bus and were ushered toward one of the planes.

Although the airplanes carried only eighteen passengers

each, I was quite surprised that each one had its own flight attendant who welcomed us on board. The inside looked even more antiquated than the outside. I sat beside a shrewd-looking Nepalese man who had taken the window seat; neither of us had much room to move. The plane was open to the cockpit, and we could watch everything that the pilot was doing. To my surprise, the flight attendant came around shortly after everyone was seated and offered us mints and cotton balls. I had no idea what the cotton was for, so I just took a mint. It seemed like a huge waste to have a flight attendant onboard just to pass around a basket of mints and then to sit at the back occupying a seat for the rest of the trip, but maybe it was a government regulation.

After the pilot had done a few tests of the engine, we started moving down the runway, and before long we were airborne. The sound of the engines was deafening, and I realized right away what the cotton balls were for: to save our ears from the loud engine noise. The noise got so loud that I had to ask the flight attendant for some cotton partway through the flight.

The flight to the Himalayan foothills took about forty minutes, and it was interesting to look out of the windows at the hills below. Nepal is an old country, so there are people living everywhere, even on the hilltops. The road systems for accessing the remote hilltop houses looked like meandering cow paths with countless switchbacks. There were farms everywhere on the landscape and small shacks where people lived. As we flew over some of the mountain passes, the plane would jolt upwards and downwards on the air currents. But all in all, the flight went fairly smoothly until the landing approach began.

The village of Lukla is situated between some very large foothills on a small, upward-sloping plateau. Just before we started our approach to the Lukla runway, we had to cross over a high mountain pass. What happened after crossing this pass was unforgettable. The pilot dropped the nose of the plane abruptly to the point where we could all see the small runway out of the front cockpit windows.

The engines immediately started to rev at a very high pitch as we continued to increase our speed, roaring downwards toward the narrow runway that was fast approaching. The runway was upward-sloping, and it terminated in a sheer cliff towering high above the valley floor. Dad, Laura, and I looked at each other with wide eyes. It sure felt like we were in a dive-bomber heading toward our target.

The runway got closer and closer, and we continued to dive until it seemed like we were going to crash headlong into it. At the last second, the pilot brought the nose of the airplane up, and we went bouncing up the sloping runway toward the small terminal. There was a collective sigh of relief as the plane jolted to a stop at the runway terminal.

As we got out of the aircraft, we could tell that the air was cooler and much fresher than it had been in Kathmandu. Lukla is at an elevation of 9,383 feet (2,860 metres). The airport tarmac was partially carved into the mountainside, and the runway sloped away from the tarmac, down the plateau, before ending at the sheer cliff.

Only a few of our bags had made it onto the plane that had brought us to Lukla, but Shera told us not to worry about the remaining bags, so we left the airport and walked around the perimeter of the airfield and on into the village of Lukla.

My knees were aching from walking down the slight incline on the far side of the runway, and again I felt sick that they might prevent me from climbing. I remember wondering what the heck I was even doing there with my knees in the state they were.

Shera led us onto the main walking path in Lukla, which was a cobblestone pathway stretching the full length of the small village, and then into one of the buildings known as the Namaste Lodge.

Inside the lodge, we went into the dining room, and Shera told us that he would head out to look for our bags when they arrived on one of the subsequent flights from Kathmandu.

The inside of the lodge's dining room was quite clean and comfortable. There was a small heating stove in the centre and many ornate wooden benches and tables around the perimeter.

We ordered breakfast from the Nepalese lady who brought us menus and some tea. The food was a tasty assortment of breads, jam, and fried eggs, which we were glad to have because we hadn't eaten all morning. After breakfast we went out into the small courtyard beside the kitchen.

By that time, Shera had tracked down most of our bags and brought them into the small courtyard with the help of a few Nepalese people who we later learned were porters. We had about eleven bags in total because we had taken Adam's bags and had also acquired another large food bag that Mom had left for us in Kathmandu.

Normally it takes between nine and fifteen days to trek from Lukla into Base Camp, and the heavy gear and supplies that are needed at Base Camp are generally brought by yaks or by zopkio, cow-like animals that are a cross between a yak and a cow. Yaks are used at higher elevations, generally above 10,000 vertical feet, because they cannot survive at altitudes as low as Lukla; zopkio are generally used at the lower altitudes.

We had started our Everest expedition later than most climbers do. As a result, all the zopkio were already being used higher up by the other climbers closer to Base Camp. For this reason, our outfitter had arranged for porters to carry our heavy supplies into Base Camp.

It was difficult for Shera to find enough porters to carry our gear, and it took a fair bit of time for him to arrange it all. Eventually, some porters showed up and started lifting the heavy bags from one place to another, piling them on top of one another and trying to make sure that all of the piles were of equal weight. We were surprised because the porters were all very small men and the loads they were seemingly preparing to carry looked large enough to crush them. There was one porter in particular who was only about four and a half feet tall and looked quite old. I couldn't believe that he was considering carrying three of our large bags, any one of which was difficult for me to lift all on my own.

We waited for about an hour while Shera and the porters spoke back and forth in Nepalese and moved the bags around to different piles at least a dozen times. Eventually, Shera told us that we should continue on without him, because they had decided there was too much weight and he needed to find another porter.

5
On Our Way

WE GRABBED OUR CLIMBING PACKS AND STARTED DOWN THE main street of Lukla. I was wearing a patella support brace on each knee to try to minimize the pain and swelling that occurred whenever I walked for any period of time, especially on downward gradients. I probably looked a little silly, and people would have certainly had a laugh at a man attempting Everest in the state I was in, but I couldn't do anything about it at that point, so I just tried to minimize the pain by taking precautions and being careful of how I walked.

On the path out of Lukla, we passed by many small shops that sold climbing gear and Nepalese trinkets, some made locally in the mountains and some from Kathmandu. Just before we left Lukla, we were stopped by a government official who made us sign some papers. The government tries to keep track of all the foreigners going in and out of Base Camp.

After descending out of Lukla the trail followed along the steep bank of the Khumbu Valley, a deep, rugged valley with a rushing river at its centre created from glacial melt higher up. The trail wound its way back and forth along the banks of the valley and was not very direct because there were a lot of smaller gullies to circumvent, created by tributaries flowing into the main waterway.

There were many small buildings along the way, the majority of which sold food and drinks and/or provided lodging to trekkers and climbers going in and out of Base Camp. These small buildings were known locally as teahouses, although most of them served more than just tea.

There were also a lot of small farms along the way, and we could see many small dirt terraces built along the valley wall for growing vegetables. However, because it was still early April, there were not yet any vegetables growing in the small terraces that we could see.

It was a very picturesque trek along the Khumbu Valley, because there was a lot of Buddhist art to see along the way. The Nepalese people paint Buddhist prayer stones, called Mani stones, and they carve Buddhist prayers into huge boulders and paint the raised letters white so they can be clearly seen from a distance.

There were also a lot of Mani wheels along the way, which are vertical cylinders of various shapes and sizes covered in Buddhist mantras and often having a bell inside. The cylinders are supported by bushings on the top and bottom ends, and the Sherpas and porters spin the Mani wheels as they pass by, causing a bell to ring inside. According to Tibetan Buddhist beliefs, spinning these Mani wheels has the same effect as orally reciting the prayer mantras written on the wheel.

In some places, the local people had harnessed small rivers and directed the water to continuously turn larger Mani wheels. This caused the bells to ring constantly as the cylinders spun.

I enjoyed the inventive aspect of these "automated" Mani wheels. It reminded me of some of the inventions Adam and I had conjured up and built over the years. We have always enjoyed putting our heads together to create new and inventive contraptions. Not all of them have been completely successful, but we have always learned a lot and had fun at the same time.

One of the more outlandish inventions we constructed when we were younger was an underwater breathing apparatus for exploring the bottom of the lake at our cottage. I got my high school shop teacher to give me an old, broken Briggs and Stratton motor, and we coupled it to another slightly-less-broken Briggs and Stratton motor that we were able to get running. Then we drained the oil out of the broken motor and filled it with vegetable oil for lubrication.

By having the running motor power the non-running motor, and by hooking a garden hose up to the exhaust port of the non-running motor, we were able to pump air down underwater. It definitely was not one of our most successful or safe inventions, though, because the motor would pump down whatever it sucked in through the intake port, including mosquitoes, dirt, exhaust fumes from the running motor, and other insects, which were not especially easy on our lungs, to be sure.

Other inventions we have built over the years include a chainsaw-powered bicycle, a homemade wakeboard, and a wood-fired hot tub.

As we passed the automated Mani wheels, I thought of these inventions and they brought a smile to my face.

I was especially careful not to do anything too strenuous to my knees as I continued on past a Mani wheel at my own steady pace. There were many places where we encountered large stone steps to clamber up or down. These places were the most stressful on my knees, and I got a sharp pain every time I had to bend them.

We passed many long trains of *zopkio* and porters along the way. The porters were all carrying extremely large loads, most towering well above their heads. Many of them were also only wearing sandals, and we saw a few wearing no shoes at all.

Almost all of the porters carried a T-shaped stick that they used as a walking stick when moving but also used to hold up their load whenever they needed a rest. Many of the sticks were carved into simple designs, and they all looked very well used. Most of the porters moved in groups, and all along the path we saw clusters of porters who were stopped and resting their heavy loads on their T-shaped sticks.

At many places along the way, the trail was carved into the side of the steep walls of the valley, and there were many long cable bridges that we had to cross. The bridges were sturdy and well supported — they needed to be, because they were being crossed almost continuously by groups of *zopkio*. The bridges would swing back and forth as we crossed them, especially if there were other porters or animals crossing at the same time.

The first day was a strenuous day for me, because I had been resting for the month prior to our departure in the hopes of healing my knee problems. By the afternoon of that first day, I was quite tired.

We knew that our first stop was to be in a little community called Phakding, about three hours from Lukla. I was relieved when we finally started seeing signs on the buildings reading, "Welcome to Phakding."

The Sunrise Hotel, where Dan Mazur had instructed us to stay, was aptly named, situated right beside the river with beautiful views in each direction. There was a large terrace in front of the hotel and a large pasture of green grass for the *zopkio* to graze.

When we arrived, we sat down at a sunny table on the terrace and gazed lazily across the river, watching for Shera or the porters. We ordered some mint tea as we waited, and we were there for quite some time before we finally saw Shera coming down the far side of the river and crossing the cable bridge.

There was electricity in Phakding that came from a small hydro power station located on one of the smaller rivers upstream of the village. However, there must have been a limited amount of electricity because there were not a lot of light bulbs, and the ones that were there required minimal power and did not produce a lot of light.

In the Sunrise Hotel, there was a sunroom beside the terrace, and that was where we ate dinner. I ordered *momos*, which are similar to meat-filled pierogies.

We decided to try a different type of tea each time we had a meal, as we slowly adapted to the new cuisine. The tea jugs have a unique design and are always the same, no matter where you order the tea. They are tall, insulated plastic jugs equipped with large corks at the top that are often coated with tinfoil.

Beyond the dining room in the Sunrise Hotel were the sleeping quarters, which branched off a long hallway. Laura took her own room, and Dad and I shared a room. There was a guy right beside Laura's room who was loudly chanting Buddhist prayers non-stop all evening and for much of the night. It was hard to spend much time at all in Laura's room, and Laura didn't get much sleep that night. I guess that is just part of getting used to the culture.

That evening, we started taking an acclimatization tablet commonly called acetazolamide, or Diamox, which is basically a diuretic to help flush water through the body. At that point in the climb, we each took only half or a quarter of a pill before bed and the same amount in the morning; as we continued up the mountain, we would increase the dose.

One important part of the acclimatization process is ridding your body of excess carbon in the form of sodium bicarbonate, which builds up inside of you when you are at a high altitude. The best way to do this is to urinate often throughout the day to help pass the carbon out of your body.

In addition to taking the acetazolamide tablets, we also drank five to six litres of water per day. You need to be drinking almost all of the time, and it is very important that you are prepared with enough water before you start climbing at the beginning of each day.

Dad had caught a chest infection in Kathmandu that was getting progressively worse. He was starting to grumble about it regularly and was upset that he wasn't able to rid himself of it. Before heading to bed, Dad and I talked a bit about the upcoming day, and I wrote down the day's events in a journal I was keeping. I was quite tired, so after our short chat, I brushed my teeth, spread out my sleeping bag, and then went to bed.

6

Up to New Heights

I WOKE UP VERY EARLY — AT 3:30 IN THE MORNING — AND could not get back to sleep. We had our morning tea and some breakfast in the dining room before heading out onto the terrace. Our porters had also woken early because they wanted to get a good start on the five-hour trek to Namche Bazaar, the village where we would be spending the following night.

It was quite interesting watching our porters preparing for the long trek ahead of them. They strapped the heavy packs onto a wedge-shaped wicker basket designed to lie flat against their backs. We were particularly interested in watching the methods of the tiny porter who had caught our eye in Lukla.

We watched in awe as he prepared his heavy load, which was almost as tall as he was, even when the basket was sitting on the ground with the stacked bags leaning up against the wall. Despite the heavy load he was preparing to lift, he was in good humour and had no problem with our taking his picture. Although he didn't speak any English, we decided to give him the nickname "Goliath" because it was truly amazing the strength he had.

I still had a lot of knee and Achilles tendon pain, but I brushed away the negative thoughts and was glad that I was at least able to trek. There were high mountains on both sides of the valley, and the trek began as it had the previous day. We passed the small, rustic-looking hydro station that provided Phakding with electricity. We also passed many more *zopkio* trains, and we learned very quickly that when passing these trains, you wanted to make sure you were on the inside of the path and not the outside, because the *zopkio* can knock you right off the narrow path, which runs along a sheer cliff in many places.

I set a fairly quick, steady pace for myself that I thought would be least detrimental to my injuries. It was a warm day, and all of us were wearing minimal clothing.

After about two hours of trekking, we came to the entrance of Sagarmatha National Park. Laura and I were forced to stop and wait for Dad at the entrance of the park because we had to fill out some documents confirming that we had a permit to enter. After Dad arrived, we spent a good half hour filling out the documents as well as trying to find and decipher the Summit Climb information from a couple of huge stacks of unorganized papers piled up on the desk in the park building. Eventually, we were given the go-ahead and were able to continue into the park.

Just after entering the park we descended quite a distance into the valley. There were huge stone steps leading down into the valley and a long cable bridge along the bottom. That particular area of the trek was very beautiful because the path followed along the bank of the rushing Dudh Kosi River. There were some sandy sections amidst the larger rocks that had been worn smooth by all the trekkers.

We ate lunch at a small teahouse close to the river that Shera had warned us was the last resting place before the very steep, three-hour climb to the village of Namche Bazaar.

We had enjoyed momos so much at the Sunrise Hotel that Laura and I decided to try them again for lunch. They said that they didn't have any meat left for the momos and asked if we would like to have tuna-filled momos instead. We thought that sounded pretty good, so we both ordered a plate full. What we did not realize was that we were far from the ocean and they don't refrigerate any of the food because there is usually no access to stable electricity. The tuna was extremely strong, and both of us felt sick to our stomachs immediately afterwards. We realized the mistake we had made a bit too late, and we hadn't even finished the plates of momos before we both had to dash to the outhouse!

We chatted briefly with some other trekkers who were quite interested in our upcoming attempt to climb Everest, and then we packed up and went on our way, leaving the small cluster of teahouses behind us in the distance.

At that point we were at the base of a very deep gorge, and far ahead of us we could see a high cable bridge suspended across the gorge, about 150 feet above the rushing river. Though it would frighten most people, we looked upon it with excitement and anticipation.

We are no strangers to extreme heights. As children we were always taught that any phobia can be overcome by mind control, and I think heights are a perfect example. There are huge numbers of people in this world who suffer from fear of heights and have suffered for most of their lives.

Phobias usually start with a scare. After the first scare, the mind remembers the fearful situation and tries to avoid it. If a person gives in to this avoidance behaviour, then the phobia gains power over him or her. Eventually, after avoiding a situation for a long enough period of time, the mind flags it as a dangerous situation and creates negative thoughts about what will happen if the situation is faced. It turns into a self-fulfilling prophecy that becomes increasingly difficult to break the longer a person lets the phobia have power over them.

Everyone experiences some sort of phobia in his or her life, but the fear of heights is one that my family has been able to control quite successfully.

Ever since a young age, Adam and I have loved jumping off high cliffs into the water and building forts high up in the trees. As we grew up, we of course started building larger and larger structures.

Another one of the inventive projects that Adam and I erected is an A-frame structure that sits on the edge of a cliff up near our cottage and hangs out over the water. The structure is more than thirty feet tall, and its sole purpose is to support a rope swing and a zip cord at its peak.

The rope swing is used by standing on the roof of a storage shed, up on the cliff, and swinging between the two upright poles of the structure until you reach the full height of the pendulum swing out over the water. At that point, the jumper is about twenty feet in the air and gets to enjoy a drop to the water below, generating quite an adrenaline rush.

The start of the zip cord is high on a tree behind the storage building, and the jumper must climb the tree to a height of fifteen feet, grab on to a pulley apparatus that is riding on the cable, and then let go and hope for the best.

The jumper then picks up speed and flies over the top of the storage shed, arriving at the peak of the A-frame structure, where the pulley stops dead, and the jumper is projected out over the water at a height of thirty feet.

The trick is achieving a vertical entrance into the water, because it can be quite painful otherwise!

The third use of the A-frame structure is as the thirty-foot jumping platform. All three of these are quite a thrill, and the first few years after we built it, we had a lot of fun trying to convince our family and friends to try them out. To this day, Adam and I haven't found anyone crazy enough to try the zip cord other than ourselves.

With the help of my uncle, we also acquired a human flat kite some years ago: a large, pentagonal kite for hang-gliding behind a motorboat. It has been great fun for us. The first few flights were a bit frightening, though, before we knew what we were doing. They haven't made or sold flat kites in Canada for many years because of liability issues, and for this reason we weren't able to find much information on how to fly; we had to figure it out by trial and error.

I remember the first time we took the kite out flying and I stupidly volunteered to try it first. It was windy that day and it was early spring, so the ice had just melted off the lake and the water was frigid cold. Most sane people would be huddled inside their cottages trying to keep warm, but we were excited to try out the contraption we had just purchased, so I suited up in a wetsuit, and we gave it a try.

The kite is permanently attached to the boat by a seventy-five-foot rope, and the pilot begins by floating underneath the kite in a square tubular frame with a bar at the front for controlling the flight. You have to wear wide skis in order to get yourself up out of the water, and you start off the way you start waterskiing.

It was quite difficult to get the kite off of the surface of the water, and it didn't help matters that most of the flotation foam had broken off to the point where the kite would hardly float. That did not stop us, though, and for about the first eight tries, I was dragged through the water, swallowing mouthfuls with every breath I tried to take.

Eventually, after many failed attempts, I was able to get up on the water skis, and down the length of the lake we went. The kite feels weightless as soon as you start to pick up speed, and I could feel it pulling up on my harness right away. We knew that the speed of the boat controls the upward force, so after getting my bearings, I signalled to Adam, who was driving the boat, to increase speed. We were heading down the lake in a tailwind, and Adam had the boat going full throttle.

I was starting to think that it wasn't going to work at all because I wasn't even able to leave the water as we sped down

*My family (L-R): Me, my sister, Laura; my father, Daniel;
my mother, Barbara; and my brother, Adam.*

Adam and Dad at the summit of Mount Aconcagua.

Standing with Dad on the summit of Mount Denali.

Dad and Mom at the summit of Mount Kosciuszko.

Dad and Laura at the summit of Mount Elbrus.

Dad, Mom, and Laura at the summit of Mount Kilimanjaro.

A portion of my personal gear.

Downtown Kathmandu, Nepal.

The small aircraft we took into Lukla.

Laura beside some of the many Mani stones on route.

Crossing a cable bridge in the Khumbu Valley with Laura.

Standing with Laura and one of the porters whom we nicknamed Goliath.

The heavy load that Goliath was carrying.

Dad jumping off of the rope swing structure at the cottage.

Flying the flat kite with Adam.

View of Mount Everest from a lookout point before Namche.

toward the end of the lake. I jumped and was able to hover for a few seconds above the water but then slowly sank back down to the surface because there wasn't enough upward force to lift me.

At the end of the lake, Adam turned the boat around, still going full throttle, to head back toward the beach. I can still remember the feeling as we rounded the corner! We were now going full throttle into a very strong headwind, and even before we finished making the turn, it happened: I was yanked vertically up off of the water and was up to about sixty feet in the air before I even knew what was happening and before Adam noticed.

The strong headwind had caused the kite to accelerate upwards at an incredibly fast speed. Adam looked back and let off on the throttle immediately, but it was too late — I had already reached close to the maximum height the rope would permit.

I had never flown before, and the kite started to swoop back and forth as I careened back down toward the water below. I was completely sideways many times, and I thought I was going to suffer an imminent crash. But luckily, at the last second, I was able to straighten out the kite and crash feet first into the water.

My heart was racing and the adrenaline was pumping through my body. I had seen my life flash before my eyes — yet all I wanted was to try it again! From that point on, we took it a little slower, and we learned our lessons about flying into headwinds. Now we can fly in all different wind types and have good control over the swooping and diving of the kite.

I think these projects and experiments have helped us develop very good coordination and an excellent ability to judge our surroundings and assess any danger so that we can adjust accordingly. We aren't the type of family that avoids any risk. Instead, we assess the risks and figure out how to mitigate them.

The climb to the start of the cable bridge in the Khumbu Valley was narrow and very steep, carved into the edge of the gorge. Although the bridge was supported laterally by cables to reduce swinging, the wind rushing down the gorge caused it to sway a fair bit. The view from the centre of the bridge was beautiful, with towering rock faces all around, so we stopped momentarily to take a few photos before continuing across. We quite enjoyed the crossing of that particular cable bridge.

On the far side of the bridge, we were greeted by a sharp left-hand turn and a steep downward climb along the edge of the sheer gorge. The trail then turned away from the gorge and began following the steep bank of another smaller river that we could hear rushing far below us.

At that point I started on ahead of Dad and Laura because I thought a quicker, steadier pace would be easier on my knees. Although Shera had warned us about the 2,000-vertical-foot climb before Namche, it turned out to be even worse than I had envisioned.

The mountainside we were ascending was so steep that the trail had to zigzag back and forth in an endless series of switchbacks. Even with the aid of the switchbacks, the path was very steep in most sections. The mountainside at that point was covered with large fir trees, so it was impossible to see how close to the top I was, and it seemed like it was never going to end as I climbed back and forth.

About halfway up that steep nightmare of a hill, there was a small plateau where I got my first glimpse of Mount Everest. It was quite intimidating to see at that point because it seemed to be a lifetime away, and I could not imagine standing on that distant peak. I could hardly fathom how we were ever going to cover the distance and elevation difference between where I was and the summit of Everest. However, it was good to finally see our objective.

The Namche climb was especially exhausting for the

porters because of the heavy loads they were carrying. There were long lines of porters along the trail, resting their weary legs, and I felt sorry for them, having to do this all their lives in order to make a living. The outdoor air and exercise would be good, but it was very gruelling work.

As I continued up the mountainside, my legs continued to get sorer and sorer until they felt like jelly, and it took all of my willpower to continue moving upward. Eventually, I got my first sight of the buildings at the edge of Namche far above me.

This gave me a bit of extra energy, and I kept moving until I finally arrived at the entrance of Namche, where I was stopped by another government checkpoint with an official who wanted to verify my papers. I didn't have any of the required papers with me, so I wearily sat down on the small checkpoint platform and waited for the others to arrive.

After I had waited quite some time they arrived, and Shera simply passed by the official while he was busy dealing with some other climbers. We followed suit and were able to avoid the aggravation.

Namche is the largest of the villages on the trek into Base Camp and is at an elevation of 11,286 feet (3,440 metres). It is a very picturesque village built into the mountainside on the saddle between two peaks. However, it is far from flat; the majority of the village is built on a thirty-degree incline.

We trudged up the steps of Namche, passing by many small shops and teahouses. The pathways were lined with flat rocks, and there was a small river running beside or sometimes underneath the pathway, in which we saw women washing clothes. We had to walk through the main part of Namche and up a lot of steep steps before we arrived at our destination, the Tashi Delek Lodge.

7
Namche Bazaar

THE TASHI DELEK LODGE WAS QUITE BASIC BUT ADEQUATE. Our rooms for the first night were in the basement, but we were told we would be moved into larger rooms on the main floor for our second night; they just didn't have any available when we first arrived.

There were two rustic-looking toilets not far from our rooms, which were located down a narrow stone hallway lit by yellowish lights on the ceiling.

We did a short tour around our new home, where we would be staying for five nights while we waited for Adam to arrive. The dining room looked nice, and it had a great view of the main part of the village of Namche below us. There were skinned animals hanging on hooks in the hallway, which was a bit of a turnoff to my appetite. However, I realized that I was probably going to see worse as we moved up closer to Base Camp. My stomach was just starting to be affected by the different foods we were eating, and I was starting to have to make fairly frequent runs to the washroom.

There was an Internet café across the path from the Tashi Delek Lodge, where they offered a very slow Internet connection via satellite. We emailed Adam shortly after arriving to let him know where we were and to tell him about what he should expect and what he should do once he arrived in Kathmandu. I was able to email Natalie for the first time since we had left Canada, which was nice, but it made me miss her that much more. The Internet was charged by the minute, so we tried to make use of the time we had in an efficient manner.

Attached to the Internet café there was also a small shop where the owner offered massages. We talked to him as we were leaving the Internet café, and after bargaining with him for a while, we were able to arrange for all three of us to have a massage. My muscles were aching, and it was good to have some of the pain relieved. I went to bed fairly early after dinner and fell asleep straightaway, although I didn't get a very good sleep, because there was a squirrel or some other creature running about above the ceiling of our room.

I woke again long before sunrise. My stomach was now considerably upset, and I felt uncomfortable because I hadn't showered in a few days. The view out of our window as the sun was coming up was incredible. Looking past the buildings of Namche, we could see many snow-covered peaks towering in the distance. We could even make out a small lodge on the edge of one of the peaks many miles away.

The lodge we were staying in was owned and operated by a local family. The grandmother of that family had a bad sickness at the time that gave her a very disgusting, gurgling cough. As we were eating our breakfast that morning, we noticed that the grandmother at the other side of the dining room was drying our dishes. As we watched her, we noticed that she was coughing her awful cough into the dishrag she was using and then drying the dishes with the same rag. We looked at each other after seeing this and felt a bit sick. I knew right then and there that I would almost certainly be getting very sick before this adventure was over.

Dad was saying that morning that he was starting to get over his sickness and it had put him in a bit of a better mood. My stomach was quite bad, so I didn't have much of an appetite, especially after watching the grandmother dry our dishes.

We moved our gear upstairs to the larger room, which had an equally great view of the village and the mountains. Unfortunately, there must have been a whole family of creatures in the ceiling above that second room, because we could hear them scurrying back and forth non-stop.

One interesting thing about Namche was the continuous "tap, tap, tap" noise that we heard all day, starting very early in the morning and continuing until dusk. This unique sound was created by the workers constructing more teahouses around Namche.

It takes a twenty-man crew about three years to construct one teahouse, and the reason for this long period of time is that they construct the teahouses out of solid chunks of rock hewed out, collected, and carried by hand from the mountainside. They chip away at the solid chunks of rock until they are able to chisel them into rectangular blocks.

All day we could hear them tapping away at the chunks of rock to create blocks, and it was amazing how smooth they could make them. They start with a huge pile of rock and work extremely long hours with basically no tools to speak of.

We could appreciate the effort that it must take to build a teahouse in such a remote location because we had gone through a similar project ourselves.

When Adam and I were in high school, Dad suggested that the three of us build a log cabin way back in the remote wilderness. A few years earlier, Dad had purchased a remote 100-acre parcel of wilderness land, far removed from civilization, and we decided it would be the perfect area for our family project. We found a suitable location on the property, a bedrock hill overlooking a small beaver pond, and we began to identify and systematically cut down the trees we would need for the construction.

We did all of the cutting in the spring when the sap was running so that the bark could be easily stripped off with the aid of a sharp axe. Unfortunately, the ideal time for peeling the bark off the trees also coincides with the heart of blackfly season in Ontario, so the bugs and mosquitoes were horrendous.

The logs were too heavy to move in the spring, so we raised them off of the ground on rocks and then left them to dry out through the summer. The following winter, we went back and were able to haul them across the snow and ice by pulling them with several snowmobiles tied together.

The following summer, we began notching the logs with chainsaws and slowly erecting the building, log by log. It was a slow and monotonous process for a lot of the time because we did not have access to electricity, and the closest road was about an hour's drive through the wilderness by three-wheeler.

It took us six long years before we finally finished construction of the log cabin but it was great when we ultimately did and could start to enjoy ourselves whenever we headed back there for visits.

It was a great learning experience as well, because we did everything by hand, right from the rocks of the foundation to the cedar shakes on the roof. We have given the cabin the name "Mallory Marsh," as it looks out onto a large beaver pond.

Back at our teahouse in Namche, we spent most of the day resting and reading on the small landing.

The teahouse was equipped with a simple shower in which the water was heated by the sun, so there was warm water only late in the day. I washed some of my clothes in the shower early on and I waited until I thought the water would be nice and warm, and then I took a shower myself. It felt so good after not having showered in a few days.

At 7:00 p.m., I wanted to try to see if I could contact Natalie, as it would be 9:00 a.m. in Canada. I went over to the Internet café and negotiated with the gentleman to let me use the Internet. Eventually he agreed, and I was able to chat electronically with Natalie over MSN. I didn't feel like eating any dinner, because my stomach was still rumbling, but Shera convinced me that I should, so I had half a plate of mashed potatoes and then went to bed.

We had planned to spend more time than normal in Namche because we were waiting for Adam to arrive. Most people spend at least two days there, because at that altitude of 11,286 feet (3,440 metres), climbers need to start to acclimatize. As you move higher up the mountain, the air becomes thinner, with less available oxygen, and you need to give your body time to adapt to these new conditions. What your body is doing is creating more red blood cells. Your red blood cells have hemoglobin, which carries the oxygen molecule. The more red blood cells you have in your body, the more chance there is that the reduced number of oxygen molecules you are breathing will be able to attach to the hemoglobin and be utilized by all of the cells in your body.

Your small blood vessels also constrict as the air gets thinner and the air pressure goes down. At the elevation we were at, the most important thing was not to go up too fast. If you do go up too fast, you run the risk of getting acute mountain sickness, AMS, which can lead to pulmonary and cerebral edema.

Pulmonary edema occurs when the small blood vessels in your lungs constrict and rupture, causing blood to leak into your lungs, leading to possible suffocation. We saw a number of people with pulmonary edema throughout the climb. You can tell if someone has this type of edema because there will be a gurgling sound in the lungs as he or she breathes or speaks.

Cerebral edema occurs when the small blood vessels in your head constrict and rupture, causing blood to leak into your brain. It is a very serious, life-threatening condition that needs to be avoided. It will often cause you to go blind, and if you don't get down to a lower altitude very quickly, it will kill you. We also saw climbers suffering from cerebral edema. They were stumbling around almost delirious and not able to control their limbs properly. In the cases I remember seeing, other climbers were helping them down as fast as possible to keep them alive. These edemas are both life-threatening conditions and are not to be taken lightly.

In the acclimatization process, it is important to expose your body to a higher altitude. This is what triggers your body to produce more red blood cells. However, it is imperative that it be done gradually, along with constant monitoring of the feedback your body is giving you.

The early warning signs of AMS are bad headaches and a feeling of nausea. A slight headache is normal when you first move to a higher altitude, but you need to be able to judge when the headache gets severe enough that you should either go down to a lower altitude or stay at your current altitude until your body has had time to adapt.

In order to expose our bodies to a little higher altitude and to remain active, on the third day of our stay in Namche, we did an acclimatization climb to a teahouse called the Everest View Hotel, which was built by the Japanese. The Everest View Hotel is at 12,600 feet (3,880 metres) in elevation, about 1,600 vertical feet above Namche. The climb was very steep and quite rocky for most of the way, but the views we got of the surrounding mountains were spectacular.

Mount Everest can be seen from the Everest View Hotel, but when we arrived, it was unfortunately completely obstructed by clouds around the peak. Dad's optimism about kicking his cold and getting healthy had worn off, and he felt even worse. No doubt that he was having the same thoughts as I: that he might be unable to continue up the mountain.

The pain in my knees had been getting progressively less

noticeable, so on our climb to Everest View Hotel, I decided for the first time not to wear my knee braces. I had some minimal pain on the way up but was able to work through it by being careful.

There is a military base on the upper part of Namche, and a helicopter landed, filling the air with dust just as we were returning to Namche. I decided to go directly back to our teahouse, but Dad and Laura made a short hike over to the military base to have a look at it.

They learned that the base had been attacked a few years prior by one of the radical political parties known as the Maoists. We couldn't figure out why they would want to take over the base, because it seemed that all they would be getting was a good view. We learned a lot more about the Maoists from Shera when he told us that they used to go around to the small villages in Nepal, seizing whatever they wanted along their way.

They would knock on people's doors and demand money. If a person did not give them money, they would take the person away from his family and make him into a Maoist. The strange and unbelievable thing is that after the election on April 10, the Maoists actually won the majority of the votes and became the party in power.

We couldn't believe how the people of Nepal would vote for such an apparent terrorist party. We asked a few of the locals after the fact, and they said that it was because the people had tried all the other parties and they were still poor and unhappy. The Maoist party promised change, which is what the people wanted, no matter how ruthless they were.

By the time we woke from our fourth rest day in Namche, it was April 12, and we were getting very tired of the village and really anxious to move on.

We received word that Adam had landed safely in Lukla and was on his way up to meet us. This was a huge relief, because often the flights to and from Lukla are delayed for days or even weeks due to bad weather. We spent most of the day resting and played cards with Shera, who was beginning to open up to us and talk a lot more.

As I mentioned earlier, yaks are not used for transporting bags in the lower altitudes because they cannot survive. They lack the sweat glands necessary to cool themselves at the warm lower elevations. Nevertheless, they are used at and above Namche, and we started seeing them coming and going in the streets of Namche. They are huge beasts and are extremely hairy, with long, sharp horns. They look like they could cause some serious damage if a person got them mad. We learned that there was not a lot of food for the yaks to eat at that time of year, so they were very weak and slow. The locals would often feed them scraps from the kitchen to give them energy to continue hauling gear.

I was starting to be able to sleep in a little longer in the mornings, as the jet lag was finally wearing off. I was now sleeping in until about 5:30 a.m. before finding myself wide awake. I was also getting into a routine with breakfast. I would usually have two boiled eggs, garlic toast, and Tibetan bread, which was a local type of tasty, deep-fried bread covered in sugar and often eaten with jam and butter.

While we were waiting for Adam, a very sick young woman arrived at our teahouse with her boyfriend and another couple. She looked like she was in physical distress and told us she had food poisoning. It was more likely altitude sickness, but she felt ill enough to call for a helicopter rescue to take her out of the mountains. Before long, a rescue helicopter arrived and set down not far from the village to take the group away.

We met some interesting people in Namche while we waited. We met a seventy-five-year-old Japanese gentleman, Yuichiro Miura, who was trying to break the record for being the oldest person to reach the top of Mount Everest. When he was seventy years old, he had been awarded the record, but a few years later, somebody older beat it. He was back to try to reclaim his title. We found out later that he did make it all the way to the top and returned back down, but unfortunately for him, there was a local Nepalese man of seventy-eight who also made it that year — an amazing feat nevertheless. Interestingly, Yuichiro actually returned in 2013 at age eighty and made it to the summit once more, once again establishing the new world record.

The same day, we also met the first Vietnamese climbing team to ever attempt Mount Everest. They were a very energetic bunch, and we became quite good friends with them, especially one of the guys who had the nickname "Loco."

Dad was still feeling very sick and was irritated that his chest infection didn't seem to be getting any better with time. We all had contracted the very bad "Khumbu cough," but Dad's was the worst at that point. At one time, he was hacking so violently that he partially dislocated one of his ribs and was in a lot of pain for a few days. He tried taking some of the medications that we had along with us in the hope of beating the sickness, but to no avail.

The day before Adam was due to arrive in Namche, Dad decided that he would go to the local Tibetan doctor. The doctor was likely not a registered physician, but he was a naturopath who specialized in organic medicines, and Dad felt like he had already exhausted all other options.

The inside of the small shop had shelves filled with jars containing small, brown balls that Dad described as looking like rabbit poop. The doctor diagnosed him and gave him some small baggies containing these brown balls. Dad was a little hesitant, but he decided to give them a try. It was actually his birthday that day, and we joked about what a great birthday present he'd gotten. He was able to treat himself to a few bags of rabbit droppings.

8

Beyond Namche

AT ABOUT 11:00 A.M. ON APRIL 14, DAY EIGHT OF OUR expedition, we finally met Adam in Namche Bazaar. We were heading down into the village and walking down one of the paths when he called down to us from a wooden balcony jutting out from the side of one of the buildings.

Adam had trekked up the Khumbu Valley to Namche along with Deha, and they were stopped at that particular building because Deha wanted to see one of his friends whom he hadn't seen for a while. Deha was not planning on continuing up with us, and after we spoke with him for a while and said our farewells, he started back down toward Lukla.

Adam told us all about the interesting situations he had encountered, arriving in Kathmandu on Election Day and trekking up the Khumbu Valley with Deha. Overall, everything had gone fairly smoothly for him up to that point, which was quite fortunate; it was a great relief to everyone that we would not be delayed any longer than we had planned for.

Dan Mazur had recommended that Adam have one rest day at Namche, but Dad, Laura, and I really wanted to get out of there and continue on. Adam did not have much of a headache from the altitude and he felt pretty good, so we decided to continue on to one of the next towns, called Pangboche, and we would take a rest day there.

Adam was a bit hesitant about this idea, but he agreed in the end after we looked at the map and the elevation difference. The important thing was that he got at least one rest day in before gaining significant altitude.

The four of us and Shera woke up at the crack of dawn the next morning and packed our bags. It was certainly nice to feel that we were accomplishing something and getting closer to our goal instead of just sitting around in the same location, as we had been doing for the previous five days.

Dad and Laura started on ahead, while Adam and I went to the Internet café to try to figure out how to activate our satellite phone, which Adam had brought along in his pack. Eventually, we were able to get the codes we needed to activate the phone, and about a half hour after the others had departed, we left the small Internet café and headed out of Namche as well.

We caught up with Dad, Laura, and Shera not long after leaving, because they were indeed going quite slowly, mostly due to Dad's chest cold. The trail was very dusty, and we had been warned about breathing in the dust, so we wore bandanas or fabric tubes called "buffs" over our mouths and noses.

The bandanas helped in two ways. First, it was not wise to inhale the dust, because the dust was largely made up of dried yak manure and it is quite easy to get sick by doing so. Second, breathing the extremely dry air in the valley was one of the main factors that cause the Khumbu cough, so by wearing something over our mouths, we could effectively help recycle the moisture in our breath and reduce the dryness.

The trail leading away from Namche followed along a steep mountainside with the Khumbu Valley on the right-hand side. At that point, the trail was high up on the bank of the valley. There were a lot of yak trains along the way, coming and going. We tried to avoid getting in their way, although sometimes this meant climbing up on to the big rocks beside the trail or climbing partway up the bank.

The trail sloped downwards for a few hours before we arrived at a small river. We ate lunch at a small teahouse near the river that had a good view of the steep, tree-covered slope on the far side.

After lunch, we crossed the river and started trudging up the long switchbacks that led up the steep slope. The ascent was similar to the ascent before Namche in that it was extremely long and seemed to go on forever. We wound back and forth up the steep mountainside until we eventually reached the top and the little village of Tengboche.

There was a large Buddhist monastery near the entrance to Tengboche, with two huge Mani wheels, each about thirty feet tall.

There were not a lot of trees in Tengboche, and the town was built on a precipice exposed to the elements, so it is almost always windy there. Although we were tired by the time we arrived, we stopped for only a short time to have a drink of water before we continued on down the far side of the Tengboche plateau into another valley.

After following the valley for a while, we crossed a bridge where the rushing river had turned the valley into a deep gorge, and on the far side of the bridge we spotted two animals that looked like mountain goats. The animals were Himalayan tahrs, and we got close to them. It was just amazing how they could cling to the side of a near-vertical rock cliff and not slip. We took a few pictures of the tahrs before continuing on.

Although my body felt reasonably good at Tengboche, we still had a long way to go, and I was hurting badly by the time we finally got to our destination, the little village of Pangboche. I remember how sore my feet were when we arrived at the Sonam Lodge in Pangboche. My right Achilles tendon was also extremely sore and painful to touch.

It had taken us over six hours to trek to Pangboche, a length of time that I was not yet accustomed to, and I was thankful that we would be taking a rest day the day after we arrived, as I felt I needed to rest my tendon to prevent further injury.

After eating and warming myself by the stove in the dining room, I fell asleep quite early.

Now that Adam was with us, he and I started sharing a room, and Laura shared with Dad. I was glad not to have to share with Dad because I did not want to catch his illness; now Laura would have to endure his coughing and groaning all through the night.

On our rest day in Pangboche, Adam and I slept in until we were woken by Laura banging on our door to get us up. I ate a hearty breakfast in the small dining room and was pleased when I headed outside and was greeted by a beautiful, clear day with minimal wind. We spent most of the day reading and relaxing on the dirt landing adjacent to our rooms, and although it wasn't a very exciting day, I was able to benefit from some well-needed rest.

The following day, we all woke up early because we needed to pack our bags for the porters, who wanted to get an early start.

Dad, Adam, Laura, and Shera went to visit a lama who lived up in the mountains. Lamas are Buddhist spiritual leaders who devote their lives to the pursuit of knowledge of the Dharma, and usually spend most of their time in solitude. The lama gave them silky Buddhist good-luck scarves and threw blessed rice on them.

I decided not to go to see the lama. Instead, I started hiking by myself toward our next destination, Pheriche, at 14,010 feet (4,270 metres) in elevation. It was not that far from Pangboche to Pheriche, although there was a fairly significant elevation gain, and I arrived after about two and a half hours of brisk trekking.

Pheriche was where we had arranged to meet up with my

mother, who had flown over before the rest of us. She had trekked up to Base Camp and was attempting to climb a nearby mountain called Island Peak when unfortunately, at just over 19,000 feet and only partway through her ascent, she had a fall that caused her to partially tear her Achilles tendon and part of her calf muscle. She was unable to continue, and she knew she would have to abandon her climbing and head down the mountain.

I walked all of the way through Pheriche, trying to find the teahouse where Shera had suggested we stay. I could not find it, and I was walking back through the village to have another look when I met a tall climber who spoke English, so I asked him if he knew where the teahouse was. He did not know where it was, but we continued talking, and I explained to him that I was trying to meet up with my mother.

I guess luck was with me at that point, because it turned out that he was staying in the same teahouse as she was. He sent me in the right direction, and eventually I heard her familiar voice calling from a small sunroom beside the main pathway.

It was a happy relief for both of us that we had finally met up, because it was difficult to organize a meeting spot in such a vast and remote area of the country with marginal communication.

Mom was quite happy that she was no longer alone, although I could see she was in pretty bad condition. Her face showed signs of wind and sun damage, and her foot was very swollen and severely bruised. She also had caught a bad illness that made her voice sound awfully raspy. The group she had been climbing with had left and continued down the mountain. It was just her and one porter named Dawa, who knew only two words in English: "up" and "no up."

There was a doctor in Pheriche, and after talking for a while with Mom in the sunroom I decided I should take her to see the doctor, so I helped her limp her way over to the small medical building. The building was primitive, although it was in better shape than I expected a clinic to be at that altitude.

The doctor looked at her foot quickly, although he didn't remove the wad of support tape that she had put on it for stabilization, and then started telling us his thoughts. He felt that as long as she made her way down the valley slowly, then she should be able to make it. When I later removed the support tape and saw her enormously swollen, purple foot, I doubted whether she would make it very far, but she decided to try.

The doctor wanted to give her some very strong painkiller drugs for the trek down, but Mom did not think it would be a good idea to take any drugs that would potentially make her dizzy as she was navigating the many treacherous cliffs on the way down. Instead, the doctor gave her some weaker painkillers that would not affect her stability or judgment.

Dad, Adam, Laura, and Shera arrived just as Mom and I were leaving the medical building. They were glad to see Mom as well and walked back with us.

We decided to stay at the teahouse where I had met Mom, because she was already established there. The teahouse was called the Himalayan Lodge, and it was quite nice compared to most, with a large dining room and decent bedrooms. It was likely a little more expensive than the one we were planning to stay at, but we were definitely happy with our decision when we found out that they served hot towels before dinner.

It was pleasant being beside the warm stove with lit candles on each table. I met some other climbers in the teahouse and played cards with them after dinner. The climbers had already been up to Base Camp but had fallen so ill that they returned down to Pheriche, where there was more available oxygen and the body could heal more quickly.

We were together as a family of five at dinnertime, and we talked as much as we could because we knew that in the morning, Mom would be heading down the Khumbu Valley, while we headed up.

9
My Mother's Unlucky Journey

AS TOLD BY BARBARA MALLORY:

Feeling alone and vulnerable on a mountain in a foreign country is hellish. I had fallen and torn my Achilles tendon and calf muscle while climbing Island Peak. My climbing partners had left me to descend the mountain, and I was supposed to meet my family in Pheriche. I had my porter, Dawa, but he kept disappearing, leaving me to hobble along on my own.

A four-hour hike turned into an eight-hour journey of pain and frustration. Finally, just before the sun dropped behind the mountains, I reached the teahouse in Dingboche.

I was too worn out to even have supper. Luckily, they gave me a room on the ground floor, since stairs would have been a nightmare. Feeling depressed and alone, I started removing my trekking gear, taking great pains to slowly and carefully remove my boots and socks.

What I saw did not make me want to do cartwheels. My left ankle was swollen and throbbing, and my left calf was a mosaic of blues and purples. I crawled into my sleeping bag, and the floodgates of my emotions opened wide. This wasn't supposed to happen. How was I going to climb with the family? How was I going to get off this mountain? I cried myself to sleep.

In the middle of the night, nature called. Like a one-legged flamingo, I hopped down the darkened hall to the washroom — an effort that left me frustrated and spent. Planting my one foot in the designated foot spot, I pressed one hand against the side of the paper-thin wall and attempted a one-legged knee bend over the squat toilet on an icy floor. Amazingly, I was successful.

The sanitary conditions, usually high on my priority list, were moved rapidly down in favour of numbing cold. I soaked my ankle in the cold wash water bucket. I would rub hand sanitizer over my calf and ankle when I returned to my tiny night habitat.

I woke to a beautiful morning with a determined heart and a newborn resolve. No one but me could get me to Pheriche to meet the family, so I thought that I had better get to it.

After breakfast, Dawa appeared from nowhere. Where he slept and ate was unknown, but he was present at that moment, and I was thankful.

We headed off slowly, hiking up the hill to climb down into the valley where the few teahouses that made up Pheriche were. Throughout the descent, I anxiously looked around for any sign of the family. I needed someone to talk to, someone who really cared. No one appeared, so I checked into a teahouse and waited.

Around 11:00 a.m., a bearded young man walked by. Even with the beard, I recognized Alan, and my heart skipped a beat. My anxiety levelled off, and I threw my arms around my son. The others would be here shortly — my security blankets were arriving.

Alan took me to the medical clinic where an American doctor gave my leg a cursory look. He asked if I wanted narcotics for the pain — NO. He gave me some very strong anti-inflammatory pills and instructions on how to use my hiking poles on my descent. I was told to descend to a lower level where there was more oxygen to help with the healing.

Because of the politics on the mountain at the time, there

was only one way down — I would have to do it myself. The family was going in the opposite direction, so Dawa, with his limited English ("up" and "no up"), would be my security blanket for the descent. This new blanket was a bit of an unknown.

I spent a very enjoyable day with my family catching up on news. Several expedition leaders gave me advice and instructed me on how to best wrap my ankle.

Well fed and well rested, I said very sad goodbyes to my family, giving them each a huge hug. I knew in my mind that what lay ahead for them would challenge each of them to the extreme and perhaps even take one or more of them from me forever, but I could not think about that. God willing, they would all return to me safely. I had to focus on positive thoughts and deal with my own challenge of getting off the mountain.

Dawa and I headed down the mountain. Through a Sherpa I met who spoke English, I had been able to communicate to Dawa that I needed him to stay with me. Both mentally and physically, I needed this dirty, frayed security blanket by my side.

Over the next four days, Dawa and I made our descent. Each night, he would direct me to a teahouse, disappear, and then show up the next morning. I shared my snacks with him, gave him some gloves, and bought him food on occasion. He was not allowed to eat with the tourists — a mountain rule.

We started to enjoy each other's company and even communicated to a limited degree with hand gestures.

On the way down, he introduced me to his sister and her young daughter. He left my side only once, which put me into a bit of a panic since he was carrying the majority of my belongings, but he showed up again about an hour later. I discovered via someone who could communicate with both of us that he had a bad toothache and had stopped to see a doctor and get some pills.

We finally reached Lukla, where I made arrangements

to fly out the next day. I gave Dawa his wages and a healthy tip and said my goodbyes to him, but he arrived the next day to accompany me to the airport. There he wrapped a yellow scarf around my neck, and we said our final farewells. I will be forever thankful to him. My dirty, frayed security blanket had been encouraging, helpful, and loyal to me.

The baggage check at the airport would not have passed the US Homeland Security standards—or any other country's standards, for that matter. An officer opened my bag, stuck his arm in, rummaged around for a minute, and then closed things up. I was soon sitting in my seat with my fingers crossed that the plane would make it off the end of the runway.

I arrived safely in Kathmandu, where Mingma, my original guide, was there to greet me and take me to the hotel. For the next several days, I wandered around Kathmandu, checked the Internet, and questioned people who were returning from the mountain or going to the mountain about conditions at Base Camp and if they had seen my family. Summit Climb, our outfitter, was getting regular reports. The family had safely reached Base Camp.

One article in the English newspaper made me quite nervous. The Chinese did not want anyone high on the mountain when they were going for the summit with the Olympic torch. The Nepalese army was up there with guns to ensure that the torch team was not bothered in any way. Another article mentioned that an American was being escorted off the mountain because of his pro-Tibet banner. Politics!

I had to make a decision whether to return home to Canada to get my leg looked at or stay in Nepal and test out their medical system. There were pros and cons to both scenarios. If I stayed, I would be closer to the family and news of their climb. I might even be able to hike back up to Base Camp if my leg improved enough; I was being very optimistic. The medical end of things worried me, however, and in the end I opted to fly home. So the frustrating "come back tomorrow" game began between me and the airline.

Finally, after much to-do, I got my airplane ticket home. I didn't have the best connections, with an overnight in Hong Kong, but who knew when or if the travel service would be able to arrange another flight in the near future? The Hong Kong airport has nice lounge chairs, and if you find a quiet area, you can actually sleep.

On the long flight from Hong Kong to Toronto, I am sure I was the subject of conversation on the airplane. Not because I was a climber and my family was attempting to summit Mount Everest but because I was afraid of clots forming in my leg. "Did you see that lady lying on the floor in the galley with her leg in the air? Why is she there? What's wrong with her?" It was an uncomfortable trip on the floor, which lacked cushioning, but the stewardess did give me a pillow for my head.

Home at last, my sister-in-law, Nancy, met me at the airport and drove me home — another security blanket.

After she left, I found myself alone again. My first job was to retrieve the dog from our friend's farm, where he had been staying. I needed company. Next, I had to see a doctor and discuss my options. My Achilles was only partially torn, and I was advised not to have it operated on if possible. Off to the physiotherapists for acupuncture, massage, and exercises.

I had to keep myself busy so as not to dwell on the fact that my family was somewhere on a killer mountain. I checked Summit Climb's website and the Mallory Expedition website two or three times a day and spoke to Susanne, our web designer, just in case Dan had sent her some info to post on the site.

I posted lots of information myself on our website: information about Mount Everest, Nepal, and my experiences on the mountain. I found this gave me a connection to the family, even though we were thousands of kilometres apart. Days passed.

Naturally, if there was no communication for a while, I would start to worry. Once I emailed Summit Climb in Nepal and asked if they knew anything about the climbers and my family in particular.

I was asked to give a short talk at Dan's Rotary club. I could do that, so I prepared a very short speech about my experience, some info about Mount Everest, and the latest news from the family.

My talk was going well, and I was keeping control of my emotions until I started to talk about the family attempting the summit in the next few days. My cheat-sheet notes started to dance in my hands, and I knew I was quickly going to lose it.

The words at the end of my notes were never uttered, and I sat down. The reality of their situation had come screaming toward me. What if? I had to stop myself from going there. I had to start cleaning house to get my mind off of things!

———

10

A Rough Night's Sleep

WE ALL WOKE UP AND HAD BREAKFAST AS A FAMILY, enjoying our last meal together on the mountain. We had taken many pictures while we were climbing up, but we did not have any with Mom in them, so we got one of the other two climbers who were staying at the teahouse to take some pictures of us.

It had snowed during the night — the first time it had snowed since we began our journey. The snow left us with some very nice views of the snow-covered fields, filled with yaks, that surrounded the village.

After we had finished taking photos, we said our farewells to Mom and watched her as she headed slowly down the mountain with her porter, Dawa. That was the last time we would see my mother until our return to Canada almost two months later.

We got an update from the other two climbers at our teahouse about the climbing restrictions surrounding the Olympic torch climb. We learned that, because of pressure from the Chinese government, the Nepalese army was displaying a strong presence at Base Camp with checkpoints and searches in place, and they were not allowing anyone to climb above Camp 1.

We were already about a week behind most of the other

climbers, who were now all at Base Camp, but we didn't feel any real need to hurry our ascent if we would not be allowed to move up beyond Camp 1 anyway. I felt quite eager to continue moving up the mountain, though, so that we would at least be in a position to continue once the Chinese had reached the summit on the Tibetan side and the restrictions were removed.

Dad was still fighting his chest infection, and he decided that he was going to take a second rest day in Pheriche. Laura wanted to stay with Dad as well to rest, but Adam and I decided that we did not want to delay and that it would be better for us to continue on up and take our rest day at the next village instead, where we would get some different scenery and expose ourselves to a little higher altitude. We packed our bags and started off at around noon, heading for another small village called Lobuche at 16,160 feet (4,925 metres).

The first hour of trekking from Pheriche was a very gradual incline through a picturesque basin where the trail ran alongside the river. There were green plants and some small flowers, which made it very nice. However, eventually the trail turned steeply upward and became quite a challenge. The river valley became more of a gorge, and we ascended until we were climbing along the bank of the river about fifty feet above raging rapids.

After a relatively short period of steep climbing, we headed down the bank of the river and crossed on a temporary wooden bridge.

On the other side of the river, we found ourselves at a small teahouse in a place called Duglha. The climbers at Pheriche had warned us not to stay at Duglha because it was smoky and unpleasant, so we had made up our minds to continue past Duglha even before we arrived.

Continuing on from Duglha, we were faced with a very steep hill to climb that rose about 1,000 vertical feet. The Duglha hill was especially rocky and exhausting to ascend. There were many different paths up the hill, all winding back and forth among loose rocks and boulders, and I was really feeling the effects of the thinner air on my body as we neared the top. We had to take numerous rest stops and stopped to eat some food on the way up as well.

Finally, we reached the top of the Duglha hill and arrived at quite an eerie area where there were about 100 memorials for many of the people who had died on Mount Everest. The memorials were mostly large rock cairns with names carved on rock slabs on the front of many of them. There were also prayer flags on many of them.

As we were trekking through, we noticed one memorial in particular that caught our eye. There was a large memorial for Scott Fischer, one of the guides from the book *Into Thin Air*, who died on Everest in the disastrous climbing year of 1996.

The wind was very strong as we were passing the memorials because that area was exposed with no protection. I had to stop and get my windbreaker jacket out of my bag because I was getting cold.

We continued on up another small valley, and eventually we walked around one of the rock jut-outs from the side of the valley to see the first few buildings in Lobuche. It was supposed to take four and a half to five hours to climb from Pheriche to Lobuche, but I guess we were moving fairly fast that day for one reason or another, because we had been climbing for less than three hours.

Lobuche was a small, dumpy-looking stopover with a few teahouses set on a dusty plateau amidst large, rocky hills, presumably created from glacial movement. Mom had used the words "armpit of the earth" when describing the village to us, so we were not expecting much when we arrived, and her description wasn't too far from the truth.

It was already late in the evening, because we had left Pheriche quite late, so we started wandering around to some of the teahouses, trying to find a place to stay the night. We went to all of the teahouses there were, one after another, but because of our late arrival, we kept finding them full. We tried every possible place, including a very expensive teahouse that Shera had told us to avoid because of the price, but none of them had any vacancy.

We were starting to get a little worried at that point because we did not have a tent with us. Eventually, we walked back through the village and entered a small lodging house for porters that we had seen on the way into the village. It was called the Kala Pattar Lodge.

The place looked like it was about to fall down any minute. It was constructed of variously sized wooden beams and metal sheeting, although the sheets were in very poor condition, with many rusted holes and parts missing.

They told us that they had room for us, and they took us through the scary-looking dining room and up a small, rickety set of stairs to a tiny hallway. The thin plywood on the floor of the hallway creaked and bent as we walked on it, and the hallway was unusually dark.

Eventually, they led us into a tiny bedroom with a handwritten sign, "Room with a View." We could not stand up in the room because the ceiling was so low, and our one tiny window looked out at a rocky ledge and a pile of scrap. However, we did not have any options other than sleeping outside, so we were grateful and decided to stay the night.

Both Adam and I felt particularly sick that night and had bad headaches, for several reasons. First, we had just ascended over 2,000 vertical feet quite quickly, so we were feeling the initial signs of acute mountain sickness. Second, we did not trust the water in the sketchy looking kitchen, and we ran out of the water we had brought with us, so we were not able to drink any fluids. And third, we did not trust the food in the kitchen, either, so all we had had for our combined lunch and dinner was a small tube of Pringles that we had split between us. But the real delight about staying in the Kala Pattar Lodge was that our room was right above the kitchen, and all night the smoke from the stove in the kitchen rose up between the tin walls and poured steadily into our room. And at that altitude, there are no trees, so the teahouses burn dried yak manure in their stoves, which created quite a foul and unpleasant smoke indeed.

These combined factors resulted in Adam's throwing up in the garbage can most of the night and neither of us sleeping much at all. We were dreadfully cold all night, and the beds must have been made of hay or straw, because they were hard and uncomfortable with lumps and bumps all over. The walls were so thin that we could hear everything that was going on in the entire teahouse. And to top it all off, we were woken up very early in the morning when Adam's bed collapsed with a loud "bang"!

Tired, thirsty, and feeling altogether miserable, we left the porter's house as quickly as we could in the morning and went looking for lodging elsewhere once the trekkers began to leave and the teahouses had vacancies once more. We found a place called the Sherpa Lodge, which had rooms available and was a significant upgrade.

After we had moved our stuff into a room and had eaten a quick breakfast, I went back to the room to try to get some sleep. I still had a bad headache from not drinking enough water, so I purified some water and drank as much as I could. I wasn't able to get much sleep, in spite of being very tired, but my headache slowly went away as the day progressed and the water in my body worked its magic.

Dad, Laura, and Shera arrived partway through the afternoon, and we all ate a late lunch together. The teahouse began having problems with their stove after lunch, and smoke was pouring out everywhere, filling the main dining room. We watched them struggle with the stovepipe for a while, and then we helped them hold and bang on the connection where the pipe went through the roof because they could not reach it.

Eventually, after removing a lot of the built-up creosote in the pipe, they were able to rectify the smoke problem, and it had dissipated from the dining room by dinnertime. I retired to our room shortly after dinner and for a little while lay in bed reading; then I tried to go to sleep, although it took me a long time to do so.

Adam and I were awakened at 4:00 a.m. by one of the members of a trekking group that was staying in the same teahouse. He was banging on our door and yelling through it in French because he thought we were part of his group. It was a bit maddening, but we just ignored him, and eventually he realized he was mistaken and left us alone.

The porters took our bags at 7:00 a.m., and we learned that they were planning on taking them directly through to Base Camp, although we would be making one more stop before we arrived there. We ate breakfast and then started out toward Gorak Shep, the last of the teahouse stopovers before Base Camp, at an elevation of 17,000 feet (5,182 metres).

The route toward Gorak Shep was quite steep in many places and also very rocky as it snaked between the huge boulders strewn about the valley. The path wound up and down, providing spectacular views of the huge, snow-covered mountains all around. I went ahead of the rest of the family, as I often had done, and stuck to my own steady pace.

11

The Last Village

GORAK SHEP IS A QUAINT LITTLE VILLAGE SITUATED ON A relatively flat ridge of earth and rock quite close to a small glacial lake. Its claim to fame is that it has the highest inn in the entire world, and it is a very popular spot for trekkers. Many trekkers will trek into Gorak Shep and climb the small peak just behind the village. The peak is called Kala Pattar, and it can be scaled in about half a day. From the summit of Kala Pattar, there is an incredible view of Everest and the surrounding mountains. We were planning on climbing Kala Pattar as an acclimatization venture, but we weren't able to get around to making it happen.

After I arrived in Gorak Shep, I had to wait for Dad, Adam, and Shera, so I decided to sit down on one of the flat rocks near the entrance to the village and study the mountains and glaciers I could see around me. I could just see the tip of Mount Everest from where I was sitting. The rest of the mountain was hidden by the other high peaks around me.

There was a treacherous looking glacier clinging to the side of the mountain walls farther up the valley. This was in fact the edge of the Khumbu Icefall, and I remember wondering how on earth we would ever be able to climb on that steep and uneven terrain. There were huge ribs of ice curled and hanging precariously all along the section I was looking at, and there didn't seem to be any realistic route that would allow climbers to pass. I stared at it for some time and remember feeling quite uneasy about the prospect of attempting to actually climb through the icefall.

After the others arrived at Gorak Shep, we went into the teahouse we would be staying at and had lunch there. The pizza they had in the teahouse was very tasty — definitely the best pizza we had had so far.

Laura had fallen sick by the time she arrived at Gorak Shep, and I was starting to come down with something as well. She went to her room to lie down, and Shera thought that she might be getting pulmonary edema, so he decided to continue up the valley to Base Camp and bring back an oxygen bottle for her. Before long, Laura was wearing an oxygen mask and feeling a bit better.

It seemed that everyone we met in the lodge at Gorak Shep was sick. At dinner, there were sick people everywhere, telling us about the awful times they had been having with diarrhea and vomiting. Some of the trekkers were so sickly that they looked as if they were nearly on their deathbeds.

I had a double bed for the first time since we had begun the expedition. It was a luxury to have at that altitude, and I very much enjoyed the restful sleep that I got.

I woke up on the morning of April 20, fifteen days into our expedition, feeling utterly sick and with a very bad headache. Dad, Adam, Laura, and Shera were nowhere near ready, so after a quick bowl of tomato soup for breakfast, I packed up my gear and headed off toward Base Camp.

The trek from Gorak Shep to Base Camp followed the lateral moraine on the edge of the Khumbu Glacier. A moraine is a long ridge of soil and rock that has been pushed up by a glacier's weight and movement and is left behind as a glacier recedes. Although the Khumbu Glacier lay to the right-hand side of the route I was on, it did not look much like a glacier at that point because it was almost completely covered in rocks from rock slides originating on the steep walls of the valley. Base Camp could be seen from quite a distance away, because the moraine was fairly high in many places. From the approach, the tents of Base Camp just looked like a few hundred tiny, colourful domes covering the uneven terrain.

Base Camp was at an elevation of 17,700 feet (5,380 metres) and was situated right on top of the Khumbu Glacier. The glacier was continuously melting and moving, so the uneven terrain was continuously changing shape as well. Much of the glacier was covered in loose rock, and there were deep caverns and small, frozen pools in many places. Base Camp covered a vast area on the huge glacier, and I estimate there were as many as 500 tents when I arrived.

It took me a while to find where the Summit Climb group had set up camp. I wandered around aimlessly for quite some time, asking many people if they knew where our expedition tents were set up, but the other climbers did not know. I had walked way out of my way to the far side of Base Camp before someone was able to finally point me in the right direction. I took a direct route, and after stumbling through many of the other expedition camps, I finally arrived.

12

Base Camp

UPON ARRIVING AT OUR CAMP, I WAS GREETED BY A FRIENDLY looking Sherpa named Temba who immediately brought me a much-appreciated cup of hot lemon-flavoured juice. I went into the yellow mess tent and sat down on one of the fold-out stools that were set up there.

The mess tent was fairly large, with about twenty stools set around a row of long tables for the twenty or so climbers who were using Summit Climb as their outfitter. There were many of the typical tall, insulated drinking containers strewn haphazardly about the tables, some containing boiled water and some containing hot drinks or hot milk. There were also small bags of drink crystals and tea.

Around the entrance was a bunch of rectangular, metallic containers which I later learned contained safety equipment and various climbing medications to help with altitude sickness and other altitude-related conditions. At the far end of the tent was a small gas heater, and although everything looked quite cramped and messy, it was a much more sophisticated setup than I had expected, as we had never had any kind of support tent on the other mountains we had climbed.

After a short rest in the mess tent, I heard some commotion outside and went out to find two other climbers from the

Summit Climb group returning from an acclimatization climb to Camp 1. The climbers were two brothers, Eric and Christian. Eric was the youngest climber in the group, at only nineteen, and I learned that his older brother, Christian, was one of the Summit Climb support doctors, although he was also attempting at the same time to summit Everest himself. I chatted with them for a while about what to expect and what had been happening on the mountain before we arrived.

Almost everyone in the Summit Climb group had already made an acclimatization climb to Camp 1, but I learned that, because of the Chinese torch run, the government was still not letting any climbers climb past Camp 1 toward Camp 2. I felt that we were quite a ways behind the other climbers in terms of schedule because we would have to remain at Base Camp for at least five days acclimatizing before we should attempt to climb to Camp 1. However, since nobody was yet allowed to climb above Camp 1, it did not seem like much of a disadvantage to be in our position.

Eric and Christian did not stay in the mess tent long before they went to their own individual tents to take off their heavy gear and get some rest. Dad and the others had still not arrived, so I decided to find out which tents had been allotted to us. I talked to Temba, and he brought me around the back of the mess tent to where all of the individual Base Camp tents were set up. He showed me where our four tents were; I chose the one closest to the mess tent and began unpacking some of my things.

The individual tents at Base Camp were sturdy, dome-type tents that had plenty of space inside for one person along with gear. They were set on top of the jagged rocks that lay on the glacier, so I was glad I had brought a few thin foam mattresses to stack beneath me. There were zippered opening on both ends of the tents and a small vestibule on one end to leave boots and other gear not required inside.

What I noticed right away was during the day, when the sun was shining, the tents were very warm. The double-layered yellow fabric of the tents created a greenhouse effect inside, and during direct sunlight, it was hot unless one or both of the tent's zippers were left open.

I lay in my tent for a time, soaking up the warmth, and after a while, Dad, Adam, and Laura arrived with Shera, and they unpacked their stuff in the remaining three tents. We were all tired and rested a bit in the warmth of our tents before dinner.

At dinnertime, Temba banged a spoon against a large pot to let everyone know that dinner was ready to be served. We went up to the mess tent and joined everyone else in the Summit Climb group who was at Base Camp at that particular moment. The expedition leader, Arnold, was still up at Camp 1, along with many of the other climbers, so numerous seats were empty.

We had salami pizza along with some boiled vegetables and other small items, and I remember thinking at first that the food was pretty good. Little did I know that, before long, I would have to practically force myself to eat it.

We chatted and got to know a few of the other members of the group during dinner.

After dinner, when the sun went down, it became cold and we had to make sure we had down-filled jackets or warm clothes on to keep from freezing. The small gas heater in the mess tent did not really have any effect unless you were sitting right in front of it.

I was continuing to feel progressively sicker and becoming more and more concerned about it, so I went to bed early to see if I could recover before it got any worse.

As I was lying in the tent, I could hear the avalanches and rock slides all around the camp. Base Camp is located within a horseshoe of very steep mountains, and there were many avalanches falling from glaciers high up on the mountainsides.

The avalanches made a sound like thunder, which could be heard all around the camp. During the daytime, they were nice to watch, and luckily none of them reached the camp because there was quite a distance between the camp and the mountains themselves.

Historically, avalanches have not been a major concern at Base Camp for this reason. However, in 2015, the earthquake that occurred in Nepal triggered a massive avalanche, which swept right across the camp like a giant wall of white, covering the area in a blanket of snow and ice. Twenty-two climbers died as a result of the avalanche, making it the deadliest disaster to date.

It was also not uncommon to hear the occasional low rumble or cracking noise as one part of the Khumbu Glacier, upon which Base Camp is built, moved against another part.

I set out my warm mountain sleeping bag as well as my fleece insert and crawled inside. I wore a winter hat to bed to keep my head warm and a bandana over my mouth to recycle some of the moisture in my breath as I slept.

I lay for a minute just thinking about where we were and what was next. We had reached Base Camp, and I was happy about that, although I knew that this was just a start and that we had a lot of difficult climbing ahead of us in the weeks to come if we even wanted to get close to the summit.

In the morning, my tent was frigid cold, and I did not want to get out of my sleeping bag. The tents remained cold until they were hit by the sun's morning rays, and then they warmed up very fast.

There was a thin layer of frost covering the inside of the roof of my tent. The moisture from my breath during the night had condensed and frozen on the tent material. This wasn't much of a worry until I started moving and discovered that every move I made would cause the cold frost to sift down on top of me. This layer of frost was common in the tents in the morning and something I had to get used to.

One of the small luxuries at Base Camp was that Temba brought a cup of hot tea around to each tent in the morning at 8:00 a.m. Unfortunately, I spilled the hot tea numerous times inside my tent while I was waiting for it to cool and trying to get dressed at the same time, but it was pleasant to have something to warm my shivering body.

Breakfast at Base Camp was usually at 9:00 a.m. during the rest days and normally consisted of Spam, cereal, and eggs. I still felt very sick at breakfast, although my headache from the altitude was pretty much gone. I drank as much water as I could during the day and tried to get as much sleep as possible in order to get myself better, but altitude weakens a person's immune system, so it is very difficult to get rid of any sicknesses. We played cards and talked with the other climbers for most of the day, and then I tried again to go to bed early.

I didn't really sleep much during the night because by that time I had very bad diarrhea, to make things worse. I woke up on the morning of April 22 extremely sick and feeling weak. I had begun coughing a lot and had a constant runny nose. I found it exhausting to do anything and hard to get enough air into my lungs whenever I took a breath.

I went to see our doctor, Christian, and after taking my temperature and checking me over, he said I had a head cold combined with a chest infection and I would need to rest at Base Camp for at least two more days. I was disappointed by this news because I was anxious to continue on and I thought if I wasted too much time getting better at Base Camp, then I would be too far behind to reach the summit within the narrow window of opportunity. However, I felt terrible all over, so I knew I could not go on.

The ideal period of time to summit, known as the climbing window, is very short on Mount Everest. Usually the climbing window is only a couple of weeks around the end of May. The reason for this is that most of the year the summit of Everest is in the jet stream, and climbing in the extremely high winds that this creates is almost impossible. In the summer, though, a monsoon comes over the Himalayas, which influences the location of the jet stream. Everest is also almost impossible to climb during the monsoon because it snows so frequently and avalanche risk is high, but the climbing window is created as the monsoon approaches. The monsoon pushes the jet stream north, creating a small window of opportunity for about two weeks before the monsoon is upon the mountain and the opportunity has passed. This is why timing is so important when climbing Everest.

Climbers start their expedition two or more months before the end of May in order to give themselves enough time to acclimatize so that they will be ready when the climbing window arrives. Although we had started our expedition a bit late, we still felt that we had enough time to acclimatize, as long as we weren't significantly delayed by unforeseen circumstances.

13

Recovery and Preparation

WE WERE INTRODUCED TO OUR TWO HIGH-ALTITUDE Sherpas, Jangbu and Sangay, who would be climbing with us above Base Camp. Jangbu was quite experienced and had been to the top of Everest several times before. Sangay had done a fair bit of climbing but had only been to the top of Everest once, and it was during a climb on the Tibetan side, not the side of the mountain we were climbing on. Jangbu was a thin, wiry Sherpa with a youthful personality, and Sangay was more heavy-set, with a big smile and a cheerful face. Neither of them could speak English very well, but we were able to communicate with them by speaking slowly and by carefully deciphering their responses.

I was too sick to move, but Dad, Adam, and Laura decided to go on without me to do an acclimatization climb, with Jangbu and Sangay, to Pumori Advanced Base Camp. Pumori is a steep mountain quite close to Base Camp, and Advanced Base Camp on Mount Pumori is at about 18,700 feet (5,700 metres). Climbing to Pumori Advanced Base Camp allows climbers to expose their bodies to higher altitude without exposing themselves to the risk of the Khumbu Icefall on the way to Everest Camp 1.

While we were below Base Camp, limiting the speed at

which we gained altitude was enough to ensure proper acclimatization and prevent ourselves from getting acute mountain sickness. Once we were above Base Camp, on the other hand, this technique was no longer adequate.

We had to change our acclimatization strategy to an up-and-back approach whereby we exposed our bodies to a higher altitude and then returned to a lower altitude to rest for a few days. Because our bodies had experienced the decreased oxygen and pressure at the higher altitude, they would continue to acclimatize and produce red blood cells even when we returned to the lower altitude to rest.

This approach of returning to Base Camp after every altitude push is necessary because it is difficult to regain much strength by resting at the camps above Base Camp, due to the extremely low oxygen levels and pressure. It is also difficult to get adequate food and supplies to the upper camps, so long periods of rest at the higher camps can be detrimental. The problem with this up-and-back approach is that it means climbing through the difficult and dangerous sections of the mountain multiple times.

I felt miserable that I was falling behind the rest of my team but reminded myself that there was nothing I could do about it except rest and hope for the best. I spent most of the day in my tent reading some of the many books I had brought along. My sickness seemed to be getting worse and worse by the minute, and I was having to run to the outhouse more and more frequently.

Although that night I had a decent sleep, the next day I woke up sicker than ever. My head felt like it was going to explode, and I was coughing uncontrollably to the point where I felt I was going to cough my lungs out. I spent another day of doing nothing but enduring my illness.

Dad, Adam, and Laura decided that they wanted to continue with their acclimatization, so they put on their gear and harnesses and headed out into the Khumbu Icefall for some practice with the ropes and ladders.

The misery I felt continued for the following day. I thought I felt slightly better in the morning, but I felt much worse again in the afternoon. I was wasting valuable time, and I was beginning to wonder if I would ever feel well enough to continue.

It seemed like everyone in the camp had some sort of sickness and almost everyone was coughing regularly. Mealtimes were a sea of germs. The general rule was that anyone who was sick had to sit in quarantine at the end of the table closest to the entrance of the mess tent. I obeyed the rule and sat in quarantine, but most people did not want to sit with other sick people even if they were sick themselves, for fear of getting worse, so they sat in the middle of the table and infected the whole group.

The morning of April 25, the twentieth day into our expedition, brought me a small ray of hope. I woke up feeling marginally better, although still very sick. I was trying to avoid all the coughing of the sick climbers in the mess tent, but it was hard to do so because everyone seemed to be hacking, and nobody was covering their mouths or taking any sanitary precautions.

I decided I would rest one more day in camp and then climb to Pumori Advanced Base Camp the following day for acclimatization. Because of their haste to acclimatize, and not knowing the route, Dad, Adam, and Laura had gone only a small portion of the way up to Pumori Advanced Base Camp when they had attempted it a few days earlier. They decided it was best to climb all the way up along with me before they attempted the climb to Camp 1. We made plans for an early start the next morning, and I went to bed immediately after dinner because I had developed a headache in the afternoon and didn't want it to get too serious.

I did not get much sleep during the night because I was very cold. Luckily, I woke up feeling again a bit better than I had the day before, and I decided to go ahead with my plan to climb to Pumori Advanced Base Camp. After breakfast, I packed my day pack and suited up for the climb.

Dad, Adam, and Laura didn't get up and get ready for the departure time we had set the night before, so I left with Sangay, while Jangbu waited around for the others.

We started out by heading back down the path we had taken into Base Camp until we reached the lateral moraine. After climbing the moraine, we headed off the main trail.

It turned out that Sangay had never actually climbed to Pumori Advanced Base Camp, so he didn't really have any idea where we were going, and of course, neither did I. Before long, we were completely off the trail, scrambling over large rocks and climbing some very steep and dangerous rock slides. A slip from where we were would result in a very nasty fall, so I was careful where I put my feet. Although we had lost the trail, I felt quite happy inside that I was at least able to be out of my tent and climbing again.

Eventually, we saw Dad, Adam, Laura, and Jangbu far below us following the actual trail, which we could now see from our vantage point. The real trail went much farther out of the way and slowly wound its way up the steep embankment.

The regular Base Camp on Pumori was on a ridge overlooking a turquoise lake, which was quite beautiful. The lake was fed by some dangerous-looking glaciers hanging ominously from the steep sides of Mount Pumori. To get to Advanced Base Camp, we had to climb a steep, rocky slope: the remnants of a giant rock slide that had occurred sometime in the past. The slope was covered in huge rocks, and I was a bit concerned that a rock above might come loose as we were climbing and claim one of our lives.

It took quite a while to get to Advanced Base Camp, as it was a long way up. When we arrived, we had lunch on the small plateau where climbers would normally set their tents. Dad didn't complete the climb to Advanced Base Camp because he felt too ill to continue; he stayed down by the turquoise lake instead and waited for us.

From our vantage point at Pumori Advanced Base Camp, we got a great view of Mount Everest and Mount Lhotse. We also got a good view of Everest Base Camp, which looked like a sea of coloured dots on the rock-covered glacier below. We could see the Everest route better from the height we were at, and we got a bit of a better perspective of what we had ahead of us.

We took a long time to get back to Everest Base Camp, and we were all very tired after the gruelling five-and-a-half-hour climb.

Upon our return, I had a shower for the first time since we had arrived at Base Camp. There were two small, narrow shower tents at the camp where it was possible to have a make-shift shower. Temba would heat up some water and put it into a plastic jug that had a hand pump on top and a small tube with a shower head on the end of it. There was very limited water, so the only way to get remotely clean was to wet yourself first by pressurizing the container and spraying a bit of water on, then shutting off the water, soaping yourself, and then doing your best to rinse off the soap with the remainder of the water in the container. It was quite a crude operation, but it was really nice at the time after accumulating days of dried sweat and stink on our bodies.

On the morning after our acclimatization climb to Pumori Advanced Base Camp, I woke up feeling much better and thinking that the sickness I had must be almost gone. This raised my spirits a bit, and it was a relief because I had thought I might have set myself back with the exertion of the climb the previous day. I did some laundry early in the morning with a pail of warm water I got from Temba. The only way to dry the laundry was to drape it on and around the tents. Sometimes it dried during the day, but often it didn't and was frozen stiff by the next morning. We took a rest day to regain our strength and spent most of the day packing and preparing for our climb through the Khumbu Icefall.

14

The Khumbu Icefall

THE KHUMBU ICEFALL IS CONSIDERED BY MOST CLIMBERS to be the most dangerous section on the southern route up Everest. The icefall is created because the upper portion of the continuously moving Khumbu Glacier, upon which Camp 1 is situated, is constantly breaking off between two large mountain peaks. As it does so, it creates enormous chunks of ice, some as large as houses, which move at four to six feet per day.

These huge chunks of ice, called seracs, are very precarious and often fall, creating ice avalanches in the icefall itself. Unfortunately, many climbers and Sherpas have been crushed by these large seracs over the years. The icefall is quite steep and technical, with a total elevation gain of about 2,000 feet (610 metres) from the bottom to the top. On April 18, 2014, a large avalanche in the upper part of the Khumbu Icefall claimed the lives of sixteen Sherpas. It was the deadliest in Everest's history when it occurred, only to be surpassed by the Base Camp avalanche the following year that was triggered by the Nepalese earthquake.

By far the most nerve-wracking aspect of the Khumbu Icefall, however, is that as the huge ice chunks are moving and breaking, huge crevasses are created that are hundreds of feet deep. These extremely deep fissures in the ice can range from a few feet across to well over thirty feet and can sometimes open or close without notice if there is a sudden shift in the ice. The deep crevasses appear to be bottomless openings which fade to black nothingness down as far as the eye can see.

In order to navigate across these numerous crevasses, the Nepalese government employs a group of Sherpas known as the Khumbu Ice Doctors to place aluminum ladders across the more than fifty chasms that are present at any given time. Many of the crevasses are too wide to be spanned by a single ladder, so the Khumbu Ice Doctors have to tie multiple ladders end to end in order to span them. The largest crevasses we saw had as many as five ladders tied together spanning them.

The ropes that are used to tie the ladders together are often very thin and frayed from having been stepped on by climbing crampons (serrated spikes that attach to climbing boots to provide increased traction on ice and snow). Because the icefall is in constant motion, the route often changes daily, and the Khumbu Ice Doctors have to go through every morning to replace the fallen or crushed ladders and re-establish the ropes and anchors.

On the morning of our first climb through the Khumbu Icefall, we woke up very early. It is important to start early because there is not as much movement of the ice when it is cold in the mornings and also because the icefall gets very hot once the sun hits it, and you want to be as far through as possible by that time. Once the ice starts to heat up and soften, it expands and can move more easily, and thus the danger increases.

We had each packed more clothes and equipment than we needed because we wanted to leave some gear at Camp 1. Our bags were far too heavy for a first pass through the icefall, and that was a big mistake.

It was still pitch black out, with a faint glimmer of light from the moon just visible on the eastern horizon, when we set out.

We were not wearing our crampons at first because we had to cross the rock-covered area around Base Camp before reaching the icefall.

It was quite awkward wearing the very large, high-altitude Everest boots that we had brought because we would be needing them higher up on the mountain. This was the first time I had worn the boots, and I was stumbling around all over the place, not helped by the heavy weight of my pack shifting back and forth on my back. This was also the first time I was attempting to climb without the aid of trekking poles. We had used trekking poles the entire way up to Base Camp because they add an extra element of balance. Without the trekking poles, I was finding it much more difficult.

Just as it was getting light enough out to see without the aid of our headlamps, we reached the edge of Base Camp. At that point we left the rock-covered area and entered onto the frozen domain of the Khumbu Icefall.

There were two officers there to make sure we had a permit to climb above Base Camp. We sat down and put our crampons on as Jangbu talked to the officers, and once we were cleared to continue, we started off again.

Although the sun was beginning to hit the mountains on the far side of Base Camp, we were in the shadows, and it was still quite cold. The initial section of the icefall was made up of many long ice ridges about ten to twenty feet high and running perpendicular to the direction we were travelling. There was minimal elevation gain for the first hour of climbing up and down these numerous ice ridges. The ice on the ridges and in the small valleys was jagged and pitted from the continuous melting, cracking, and movement of the icefall.

I felt, and must have looked, very awkward going up the steep ridges because I was favouring my Achilles tendons by climbing the slopes with my feet splayed outwards like a duck or by climbing up sideways. This was to ensure that the weight

Looking down at the teahouses in Namche Bazaar.

Workers constructing a teahouse in Namche Bazaar.

Dad and Mom in front of our log cabin, "Mallory Marsh".

Yak used to carry gear to and from Base Camp.

Long line of yaks carrying goods.

Mom ascending a fixed line on Island Peak.

The whole family together at Pangboche.

In front of porter's lodging house in Lobuche.

Gorak Shep with Kala Pattar in the background.

Approaching Base Camp.

Interior of one of our tents at Base Camp.

Mess tent with other climbers in Summit Climb group.

Washing and drying clothing at Base Camp.

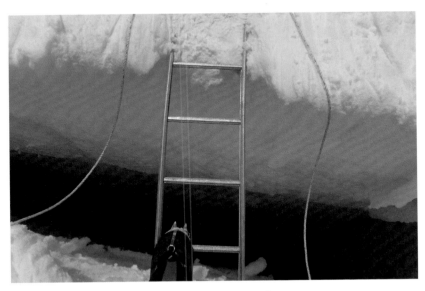

Looking down into one of the smaller crevasses.

String of ladders across a deep crevasse.

The beginning of the Khumbu Icefall.

of my body and pack would be transferred through the sides of my feet instead of through my Achilles tendons. By reducing the number of times I had to go up on my toes, I was able to reduce the pain and swelling. However, there were many places where sideways climbing was not possible, so I could not avoid toe-point climbing the entire time.

After the first hour of climbing in the icefall, the route became quite technical. The icy path began to slope upwards, and we started to see the enormous seracs all around, looking like they were ready to fall on us at any moment. The route snaked its way between the huge seracs; in many places, they hung precariously over where we were climbing. We could see the aftermath of ice avalanches everywhere, and the inherent danger of the icefall was quite vivid all around us.

Eventually, we started to come across small fissures in the ice beneath us that we had to step over very carefully. Looking down into the fissures was eerie, because all we could see was the hollow darkness below. The higher we climbed, the wider the fissures became, and before long we came to our first ladder to cross.

Although I knew that the ladders existed and that we would eventually have to cross them, there is a difference between imagining what they would be like and actually physically doing it. The first ladder we came to was a single ladder, meaning it was not tied end-to-end to another in order to bridge the gap, and it was fairly level. I was glad of this because it gave me a chance to practise over a short distance before attempting the very long ladders, which I knew we would be coming upon shortly.

We were all wearing climbing harnesses over our down jackets and pants, and attached to the front of our harnesses was a length of webbing: a strong, woven fabric in the shape of a flattened tube. The webbing was attached to our harnesses by a knot in the centre, leaving the two ends of webbing extending out about three feet on either side of the knot. Although we had brought a lot of carabiners and other climbing hardware with us to Base Camp, Jangbu and Sangay suggested that all we would need was the length of webbing, one carabiner, and a Jumar ascending device. We had attached the carabiner and Jumar to the two ends of webbing, and it was great not to have to carry a lot of extra equipment on our harnesses.

The Jumar ascenders that we were using had a spring-loaded cam with teeth that was designed to slide freely on a rope in one direction but to hold fast to the rope when a force was applied in the opposite direction. We had used these types of ascenders in the past, and they had worked well.

On the sides of most of the ladders there were two loose ropes that were used as a safety backup in case the ladders failed or in case one of us lost our balance and plummeted into one of the crevasses — a very real possibility. Before crossing, we would attach our ascending device to one of the ropes and our carabiner to the other.

I was the first to cross this initial ladder that we encountered, and it was quite a slow process crossing it. After attaching my Jumar and carabiner to the safety ropes, I stepped out onto the start of the ladder. The ladder made a creaking sound as I transferred my weight to the first two rungs.

The most challenging part was balancing my heavy pack while I stood on one foot to move my second foot forward to the next ladder rung.

After that second step, I was fully suspended over the crevasse on the small aluminum ladder. Although I knew I probably shouldn't look down, my curiosity got the better of me and I stared down into the empty blackness below. Wow! That was living on the edge, and I felt a surge of adrenaline. I continued slowly across the ladder in the same fashion, one rung at a time, until I was able to step off the far side onto the hard ice once more. I stopped on the far side to watch the others cross.

As we moved higher up the icefall, we encountered more and more ladders, which were longer and more precarious. Many of the ladders along the way were not level but were angled either upwards or downwards, and some were even tilted sideways. The ones which were tilted sideways were the most difficult to cross because our metal crampons would often slip sideways as we were crossing.

An even greater problem with the crampons was that if we didn't put our boots in the exact right spot on the ladder, the serrated metal spikes of the crampons would often lock onto the ladder rungs. I cannot think of anything more frightening and exhilarating than that situation. We would have no choice but to steady ourselves on the ladder as much as we could and then attempt to yank the stuck foot free with a well-timed jolt or twist of the appropriate leg. This sudden movement would cause the entire string of ladders to bounce up and down while we frantically tried to regain our balance. Often the crampons' spikes would get wedged around the ladder rungs so tightly that it would take many tugs in order to free them. Hovering above a seemingly bottomless crevasse trying to free a stuck crampon in that way was quite an interesting experience.

Despite the dangers and many tricky sections in the Khumbu Icefall, the views were breathtaking, and the challenging route was exhilarating. There were several vertical climbing sections along the way, many of which were quite technical. The route was mainly made up of steep upward climbing, although at times we had to descend into deep ice gullies along the way before climbing out the other side.

We saw many avalanches cascading down the steep mountain slopes on either side of the icefall. These avalanches would race down the slopes and crash into the periphery of the icefall, making a loud noise like thunder and sending up a huge white plume of snow and ice. There was one area in the icefall where the route got quite close to one of the mountain slopes, and I tried not to think of what would happen if an avalanche were to come down while we were passing through that particular area.

After four or five hours of continuous climbing, the sun was high enough in the sky that its rays fell upon the icefall and the temperature went from being very cold to very hot. The reflection of the sun off the huge ice seracs all around made the heating and lighting effects of the sun very powerful.

At higher altitudes, there is not as much atmosphere to filter the rays, so the sun is extremely intense, and we needed to make sure we were wearing our glacier glasses the entire time, or we would surely get snow blindness.

I did not take snow blindness lightly because I had had a very scary experience while climbing Denali four years earlier. On Denali, I had taken my glacier glasses off for a short period of time while I was making dinner because the sky was overcast and it did not seem very bright to me at that time. Although it did not affect me at first, shortly after dinner, when I was getting ready to go to bed, my eyes started burning and I could not look at anything bright. Denali is in Alaska, and we were climbing in the summertime, so we had twenty-four hours of daylight. The burning in my eyes kept getting worse, and soon I could not keep them open even in the tent. By the time I tried to go to sleep, even the light penetrating through my eyelids was too painful to handle. I had to wrap a bunch of my clothes around my head to block out all light. It was frightening to think I was going blind and I would have to be rescued off the mountain. Luckily, by morning, the pain had dissipated, and my eyesight was normal again. I had learned my lesson, and it was one I would not forget.

In addition to making sure our eyes were well shielded in the icefall, we also had to worry about the exposure of our skin. The intense sunlight at high altitude burns climbers' skin very fast, and we needed to be constantly monitoring ourselves and each other to make sure our skin was not exposed. As well, we needed to frequently apply strong sunscreen on any skin that was not completely covered.

There are areas of the body that you would not normally think of as at risk of burning. For example, the reflection of the sun off of the ice and snow actually burned the insides of our nostrils and the roofs of our mouths if we were breathing heavily with our mouths open.

There were fixed ropes along the route through the icefall, and the ropes were anchored (in places where it was possible to anchor them) either by aluminum stakes pounded into the ice, which were the most common, or by ice screws. The problem that we discovered before long was that the anchors created a bit of a false sense of security.

A few times, one of us would pull against the rope, and the anchor would pull right out of the ice. The sun's rays heated up the aluminum anchors, melting the ice around them and rendering them useless, in many cases, if there was any amount of upward force applied.

Hour after endless hour, we continued to climb up the icefall. Dad, as he was still feeling weak from his chest infection and had dislocated a rib the night before from coughing, had fallen behind with Sangay. His condition was quite debilitating. All of us were dealing with our individual physical challenges in our own way while looking out for each other as best we could.

Laura and I had gone ahead with Jangbu, and Adam was climbing by himself somewhere in the middle. I was leading, but I was beginning to move very slowly because my legs felt like putty and my muscles burned with every step.

After about five or six hours of climbing, we met a team coming down, and I asked them how much farther it was to Camp 1. They looked at how exhausted we were, and knowing the area of the icefall that we were in, they advised us to head back down. This was disheartening because I knew it meant we had a long way still to go and I was already completely spent. However, I was determined, as was the rest of the team, so we continued at the snail's pace we could maintain.

There are a few particular sections in the icefall that I remember quite clearly. About halfway through, there was a section where there was a very high vertical ice wall that we had to scale. The wall was about forty feet high, and there were five ladders stacked vertically end to end and tied precariously one above the other, reaching the top of the wall. Struggling up that mess of ropes and bent ladders was quite an experience.

The second section I remember quite clearly was a very wide crevasse near the top of the icefall where the gap in the ice was about thirty-five feet across. There were four ladders tied end to end in order to bridge the enormous gap, and there were many ropes going through the ladder rungs and attached to the sides of the crevasse to add support. The string of ladders was on about a ten-degree slope upwards, to make things even more difficult, and the safety ropes were very taut because the crevasse had clearly continued widening since the ropes had been put in place. When I arrived at that crevasse, I was a fair distance ahead of Jangbu and Laura. I knew there was no turning back, so I clipped in to the safety ropes and started across.

The ladders began to creak and sway from side to side and bounce up and down with every step. My heart was pounding very fast in my chest the entire time. It took me a long time to cross, and there was, of course, no place to rest halfway. It also took a lot of energy to balance myself for that long period of time, and my legs were shaking uncontrollably from the lactic acid buildup by the time I reached the far side. I remember thinking what a relief it was to be across that ladder, although I was also dreading having to return across it on our climb back to Base Camp the next day.

The last ascent at the top of the Khumbu Icefall was probably the most technical section of all. It required us to climb another string of five ladders up a huge ice face and then traverse a small, icy ledge. The ledge sloped upwards and led to another near-vertical ice wall, this time with no ladders for the majority of the way up.

We had to climb the steep ice wall by digging the toe points of our crampons into the ice until we could eventually grab on to a short ladder hanging from the top of the ridge. I remember how painful it was for me to summon up enough energy to lift my body up onto the hanging ladder and then climb straight up onto the ridge above. When I got to the top, I could see that I was finally out of the icefall. I took off my pack and collapsed onto the ice to rest.

By the time I had reached the top of the icefall, I had entirely "hit the wall," which is to say I had completely exhausted all of my energy stores. I lay on top of the thin ice ridge and watched Laura and Jangbu, who had just arrived at the thirty-five-foot crevasse far below. I took a video of Laura crossing the ladders, and she looked just as terrified as I had been.

I was enormously relieved that we had finally reached the top of the icefall. It was incredibly hot from the sun reflecting off of the ice, and all I wanted to do was to arrive at Camp 1 because I could hardly move and I desperately needed rest.

I lay on the ice for about twenty minutes until Laura and Jangbu climbed the final ice wall, and then I forced myself to get up and continue climbing along with them. Every step was exhausting and difficult because my body was completely out of energy. I had thought that when we reached the top of the icefall we would be at Camp 1, but my spirits sank even lower when I found out from Jangbu that we still had a long way to go before we would reach the camp.

Above the Khumbu Icefall, we were entering the area known as the Valley of Silence or Western Cwm — *cwm* being a Welsh word for a valley. The area was named by George Mallory, the first to arrive in the area in 1921. I will explain our connection with George Mallory near the end of this book.

Nestled within the steep mountain walls of the Western Cwm lays the upper expanse of the Khumbu Glacier, spread out like a giant blanket of white amidst the towering peaks that surround it. Although that portion of the glacier did not have the steep vertical rise of the icefall, it had its own challenges. It was arguably safer because there was less risk of ice avalanches and less movement of the ice beneath our feet. However, it was still a very risky and difficult area, because the Khumbu Glacier was covered with extremely deep and expansive crevasses, many of which stretched right across the glacier from one mountain wall to the other.

There were long ladders in place traversing many of the crevasses, but there were also numerous crevasses that were too wide to traverse with ladders. These we would have to climb down into and up the other side. The routes down and up these very wide crevasses were often especially technical, and many times there were ladders on the vertical ice faces inside the crevasses to allow climbing up and down the interior ice walls.

Much of the climb through the Western Cwm was spent winding between crevasses on very thin ribs of ice, which added a lot of extra distance. At one point, the route carved dangerously close to the side of the Western Cwm, where it was very near to the base of the steep mountain wall. There were huge ice seracs clinging precariously to the wall above us at that point, and if one had broken off, it would have surely reached where we were climbing. I wanted to go through that particular section as fast as I could, but my body was so exhausted it was a very slow process.

Jangbu, who was in much better condition than we were, was having to wait while we lay on the ice, exhausted, between each of our very short spurts of movement. Laura and I continued, trudging along one slow step at a time. And after what seemed like an eternity, we finally got a glimpse of Camp 1.

The many crevasses that we had encountered on our journey through the Khumbu Icefall and across the upper span of the Khumbu Glacier were certainly not for the faint of heart, but they weren't the first crevasses we had ever encountered, which added to our confidence a little. In 2004, when Dad and I were climbing Denali, we had a similar but also quite different experience with crevasses.

For about the first half of the climb on Denali, we were climbing along the massive Kahiltna Glacier, which is the longest glacier in the Alaska Range. Naturally, there was a myriad of active crevasses on the Kahiltna Glacier, but what added to the danger was that the blowing snow on Denali would cover them up, creating a snow bridge so that from the surface, there was no way of knowing where the crevasses were.

If the snow bridges were strong enough, climbers would pass overtop without even knowing that there was a crevasse beneath them. However, sometimes the added weight of a climber was more than the snow bridge could support, and the snow would give way, causing the startled climber to fall hundreds of feet to the bottom of the crevasse — and this would usually claim the climber's life as well.

For this reason, on Denali we were roped together so that if one of our team members unexpectedly fell into a crevasse, then the rest of us would perform a self-arrest and then work to rescue the fallen climber. A self-arrest involves falling onto the snow or ice with your ice axe held across your chest so that your weight forces the pick of the axe into the snow or ice beneath you. Simultaneously, you drive the toe points of your crampons into the snow or ice, essentially creating a three-point human anchor that will allow you to break the fall of the plummeting climber connected to you by the climbing rope. The manoeuvre has to be done quickly and effectively so that the weight of the falling climber does not catch the rest of the team off guard and pull them all into the crevasse — a very tragic event that has happened in the past.

Once the fall has been halted, the challenge is to rescue the fallen climber, who at that point is suspended from the climbing rope and dangling in the dark crevasse below. If the climber is still conscious, he or she can often climb out of the crevasse using loops of cord and a specific knot known as a Prusik knot to slowly ascend the climbing rope. However, if the fallen climber is unconscious or injured from the fall, the rescuing climber or climbers have to create and utilize what is known as a Z-pulley system to hoist the fallen climber back to safety.

We were equipped for all these situations and had practiced the rescue techniques, but fortunately we did not have to put them into practice on any of the crevasses on Denali.

We did have a very serious situation on the Kahiltna Glacier, though, where we almost lost my father forever. It was a section where we were mistakenly not roped together, and Dad punched through a snow bridge with both feet. Thankfully, the snow bridge did not collapse completely, and his pack caught on the remaining snow, allowing him to pull himself out of the crevasse to safety.

It was a silly mistake we had made, not being roped together for that particular stretch, which was on the way down after we had reached the summit. We learned our lesson, though, and immediately roped up and put on the snowshoes we had brought to increase the surface area bearing our weight and decrease the possibility of breaking through any additional snow bridges ahead of us.

15

The First Camp

CAMP 1 WAS SET UP RIGHT ON TOP OF THE UPPER PART OF the Khumbu Glacier, at an elevation of 19,900 feet (6,065 metres). The tents were perched on top of two very wide ice ridges separated by the remains of a wide crevasse that had been partially filled in with snow and ice to the point that it looked more like a deep gorge spanning the glacier.

When I finally arrived at Camp 1, I immediately went into one of the closest tents and collapsed. I had pushed my body way past its energy limit, and every muscle in my body was sore and exhausted from more than eight arduous hours of climbing.

After a short while, Laura and Jangbu arrived, and eventually, Dad, Adam, and Sangay arrived at the camp as well. All of us were completely depleted and lay in our tents, not able to move.

Thankfully, Jangbu and Sangay, who were sharing a tent, made us each a cup of warm soup, which was so appreciated because the last thing we wanted to do at that point was to go out looking for some clean ice and snow to gather for melting and boiling in the tent.

We had learned previously that because Camp 1 is quite open and exposed to the elements, it is a very cold and windy place to stay. Shortly after we arrived, the wind picked up, and we experienced it first-hand. Even the very sturdy climbing tents that we were in were shaking and partially collapsing in the strong gusts. Dad, Adam, Laura, and I used our small hand-held radios to communicate with each other so that we wouldn't have to go out into the strong winds or move any of our tired muscles.

There wasn't really a toilet at Camp 1, although we figured out that everyone was trying to make sure that they went down into one of the ice gullies and not on top of the ridge. The first time I had to go to the washroom, I could see where someone had built a small wall of snow to designate the washroom spot. It was difficult, however, to get down into the valley because without crampons on my mountaineering boots, my boots acted like skis on the ice and snow. I slipped many times on the way down, narrowly missing a pile of human waste at the bottom. It was a cold and unpleasant experience, to say the least.

I tried to stay in the tent as much as possible for the rest of the day. I went out only a couple of times to collect ice and snow to replenish my drinking water supply and for making more soup. The rest of the time was spent tending to the small gas cookstove that hung from the vestibule at one end of the tent. The stoves were designed to hang from a string or wire, and they each had a small, removable metal bowl that sat on top. They used special high-altitude pressurized gas cylinders, because normal stoves do not work up there due to the lack of oxygen and the low air pressure.

All the water we drank had to be boiled first to prevent us from getting sick. Although the glacier ice and snow itself is very clean, it basically never melts up at that altitude, so there is always the possibility that it has been contaminated by other climbing groups in past years.

A huge amount of time during the expedition was spent

in this manner, melting ice and snow. It became a necessary daily ritual.

It reminded me of making maple syrup at the cottage. In a similar fashion, we would spend countless hours boiling the maple sap after collecting it from the many buckets hanging from our maple trees.

It takes forty gallons of sap to make one gallon of maple syrup, so it was always a time-intensive activity. Growing up, we usually made maple syrup every two years, and we tapped and hung sap buckets on around fifty trees when we did. It was a valued family tradition that brought us together, and it was often a lot of fun waking up early and taking the snowmobiles out into the forest to collect the sap from the buckets.

As kids, my siblings and I used to really like drinking sap from the buckets before we poured it into the collection tank. The boiling part was interesting as well. We had an old cast-iron cauldron that Mom had acquired, and that is what we always used until recently, when we were given a small but more advanced evaporator unit. I preferred the cast-iron cauldron method, though, because it was much more of a rustic and traditional experience.

We hung the cauldron over a fire from a chain attached to a homemade log support structure and stacked the firewood around the base of the cauldron. Once the fire was started, we often left it for a few hours at a time to go do other winter activities. The only trick was to make sure that the sap level did not boil down too low, or it would start to turn to maple sugar. To prevent this, someone had to check on the cauldron every few hours to add more sap to the mix as needed. It was often a very social time as well, because our aunts and uncles would join in the process and sometimes our friends would help out as well when they were visiting.

With this memory of home in my mind, I curled up in my sleeping bag and attempted to fall asleep. Although the powerful wind was constantly beating the sides of the tent and it was an uncomfortable place for sleeping, I was able to fall asleep quite early because of my utter exhaustion.

It was a difficult, cold sleep, mainly because the ice at the bottom of my tent had melted into a bowl shape from the sun and other climbers that had used the tent previously, and I was not lying flat at all.

In our tents in the morning, we each had breakfast consisting of a bit of cereal and powdered milk in a tin cup. The breakfast was not at all satisfying or the least bit tasty, but we needed the food for energy, so we forced it down.

We had decided previously that we would make an attempt to go to Camp 2 so that we could expose our bodies to the higher altitude and speed up our acclimatization. We were not planning on staying at Camp 2, because it could be dangerous to stay at that altitude before we had time to properly acclimatize. We decided to stick to our plan in spite of our sore, tight muscles. And so, shortly after breakfast, we put on our gear and departed.

We had taken almost all of the equipment and supplies out of our bags so that we would have less weight, and we did not really need anything with us because we would be coming back past Camp 1 a few hours later.

It took some time before my muscles were functioning properly, but amazingly I had regained some of my strength. It is incredible how the human body can recover after a short night's rest.

After going down into the belly of a deep crevasse, the route angled upwards and became fairly steep for some time as it began following along the base of a very steep-sided mountain called Nuptse. The route was in that location to avoid the countless huge crevasses across the centre portion of the

Khumbu Glacier. However, there was evidence of many avalanches dropping off of Mount Nuptse that swept right across the trail, so we had to be careful.

There was an elevation gain of only about 1,300 feet (396 metres) between Camp 1 and Camp 2, and most of the gain was in the initial steep ascent. At the top of this ascent, we could see Camp 2, although it was still a good distance away.

There were ladders to cross along the way, and we continued to wind around and between many deep crevasses. I remember one of the ladders in particular that was quite treacherous because it was not sitting flat. The beginning and end of the ladder were at the same elevation, but the ladder itself was tilted sideways, so when I stepped on a rung, my crampons and boots would slide sideways to the edge of the ladder. That particular ladder was comprised of two sections tied together and was especially challenging to cross.

After reaching the top of the first steep ascent, about half of the distance to Camp 2, and already fatigued, Adam and I decided that we would return to Camp 1. We had already accomplished the majority of our planned elevation gain, and we both had pounding headaches from the altitude, so we thought it would be wise to turn back. Dad and Laura decided to continue on, although Dad also turned around just before reaching Camp 2, and Laura was the only one of us who actually went all the way before returning to Camp 1.

When Adam and I arrived back at Camp 1, it was around noon, and we made ourselves lunch using the stove hanging in my tent. We boiled some water, and each of us had two packets of dried noodle soup, which I will say tasted very good at the time. I developed an even worse headache in the afternoon, though, which did not go away, and I was very glad that Adam and I had made the decision to turn back when we did.

Dad and Laura returned later in the day. They had gone much farther than we had, but their decision to continue may not have been a good one. They arrived feeling completely depleted, to the point where they were on their last legs when they reached us. Dad was extremely sick with his ongoing chest infection that was causing him to cough uncontrollably for extended periods of time, and Laura was coming down with a similarly severe sickness as well.

The winds were relentless all day, and sometimes the gusts were so strong that they flattened the roof of my tent, pushing it down on top of me where I was sitting. Most of the remainder of the day we spent melting ice and snow to replenish our drinking water supplies. Hour after hour, I kept melting snow and ice on the small stove to create a sufficient amount of water for the next day.

Camp 1 had not always been in the same location. In fact, in previous years, Camp 1 used to be lower on the glacier, closer to the upper limits of the icefall. Jangbu told us that a chunk of ice broke free and fell from high on one of the adjacent mountains, resulting in an avalanche which cascaded down toward the old location of Camp 1 and swept right across the Western Cwm, wiping out almost all sixty tents that were there at the time. Miraculously, nobody was killed in the disaster. It was late in the climbing season, so most of the climbers were elsewhere on the mountain.

Jangbu was the first person on the scene that morning after the avalanche, because he was climbing up the icefall very early. He couldn't believe what he saw when he arrived, because Camp 1 was all but destroyed. All he could see was debris, shredded tents, and the arms and legs of the few climbers who were staying at Camp 1, struggling to get free. Luckily, he was able to help dig them out. It really was a miracle that there were no fatalities, although there were broken bones and other injuries to contend with.

After the avalanche, the location of Camp 1 was moved higher up the Western Cwm, but there is no certainty that the new location of Camp 1 is any safer. This is one of the main reasons climbers try to avoid staying at Camp 1 after their first acclimatization push up the icefall. The other reason is that the high winds make it quite a miserable area to spend much time.

During subsequent climbs up the icefall, most climbers attempt to climb all the way from Base Camp to Camp 2 in one day. This is quite a long distance and very tiring, but we decided we would eventually try to do this as well, to avoid the exposure at Camp 1.

After our second night of restless sleep at Camp 1, we felt miserable and needed to get lower on the mountain for some recovery time. I woke up early so that we could descend through the icefall before the intense sun bore down on us. Unfortunately, we got a very late start, as Dad and Laura were feeling very weak and were not as concerned as I was about getting through the icefall early.

We left almost all of the gear we had brought up with us through the icefall. There was a designated gear tent at Camp 1 that we were able to leave it in. Then we started heading down with nearly empty packs.

It felt good to be going down, and Adam and I felt quite strong because we had rested most of the day before and we had very little weight on our backs. The only weight we had was the water we knew we would need on the climb down and a few other essentials.

We crossed the ladders and deep crevasses below Camp 1 and arrived at the crest of the Khumbu Icefall at about the time the sun's rays were just starting to reach the top of the icefall. This meant that we would have about an hour of shade before the entire icefall would heat up with the intense rays of the sun. All four of us were together at that point, along with our two Sherpas.

The very technical section with the vertical hanging ladder at the top of the icefall was much easier on the way down because we were able to bypass most of it. There were two well-secured abseiling ropes hanging down from the vertical ice face for descending. We were able to clip into these ropes, and using our figure-eight rappelling devices, we rappelled vertically down the ice wall into the icefall below. It was exhilarating and saved us a lot of time.

At the bottom of the ice wall, we came across two men from the Nepalese army who were heading up the icefall destined for Camp 2. One of them had a long container strapped to his back, and Laura asked him what it was. He replied in broken English that it was a rifle. She asked him why he was bringing a rifle to Camp 2, and he replied that they had been instructed to shoot anyone who attempted to climb past Camp 2 before they were given permission by the Chinese government to do so. It was evident that the Chinese government was taking this issue very seriously, to the point where they would rather take someone's life than be exposed negatively in the media.

As we continued down the icefall, it became warmer and warmer. And before we were halfway through the icefall, the intense sun was shining directly on us. I went on ahead of the others, because they were moving slowly and I wanted to minimize my exposure, especially now that the icefall was warming up.

Even descending through the icefall was very difficult because of the large number of long ladders to cross and the continual climbing in and out of small valleys and up and down ice ridges. I was again completely spent by the time I reached Base Camp. I staggered into camp and rested in the mess tent until Adam and Laura arrived and, later, Dad, who was now sick as could be and had nearly completely lost his voice.

16

Rest and Recovery

DAD DECIDED HE NEEDED TO GO TO A LOWER ALTITUDE where the increased oxygen would help speed up his recovery. Although I was unsure of this strategy and didn't want to risk losing the acclimatization benefits we had gained, we all agreed to go down with Dad.

The idea of going down and spending some time at a lower altitude did have a certain appeal, because the political situation was no better and climbers were still not allowed to climb past Camp 2. We wanted to use the Internet, which was available farther down, in the village of Dingboche, and we were also looking forward to some different food. The food at Base Camp was becoming very monotonous. It was often out of cans, and I got very bad heartburn every day and had to start taking Zantax and antacids to relieve the acid reflux.

After a good night's rest, we packed the basic necessities that we needed to bring with us and started heading down. I felt quite strong all the way down to Gorak Shep and then through to Lobuche. It was about five and a half miles (nine kilometres) down to Lobuche, but we were moving at a very fast pace because of the increased oxygen levels. We had lunch at Lobuche, and after a quick bowl of soup, we continued heading down because we wanted to make it all the way to

Dingboche, which was ten miles (sixteen kilometres) in total from Base Camp.

Long before arriving at Dingboche, I developed very bad pain in my Achilles tendons and calf muscles. It was an extremely long day, and by the last section, I had slowed to a snail's pace. The rest of the family and Jangbu went on ahead of me, and I plodded along with very short steps to try to minimize the injury I was causing.

The latter part of the route down to Dingboche was more direct than the route we had come up from Pheriche. The route traversed the side of a steep mountain and eventually arrived at a deep green valley, within which the village of Dingboche was located.

By the time I had limped my way down the side of the steep valley and found the teahouse we were to stay in, I just collapsed on the bed and spent at least an hour there before I could attempt to move again.

We stayed at the Valley View Lodge in Dingboche. It was nice to have a bed to sleep in again, even though it was very basic. The food was certainly a refreshing change from the food we were getting at Base Camp. We were able to choose from an assortment of different dishes, including yak steak and other meats and vegetables that were a welcomed variation for our palates.

Jangbu joined us for dinner that night. It is interesting to watch the Sherpas eat. They almost always eat a dish called dal bhat, which is rice with lentils and sometimes has some meat mixed in as well. Dal bhat was not very appealing to me, but they say it gives them a lot of energy.

One interesting thing about the Sherpas is that they don't use utensils when they eat. Instead, they always use one hand to move the rice or other food from the plate to their mouths. One would expect such an eating method to be rather messy, but they are able to do it neatly and rapidly without spilling their food. We noticed that they use only their right hand to eat, and we later learned that the reason for this is because their left hand is used to splash water on their backside after using the lavatory. I remember thinking that it's a good thing I always shook the right hand of the Sherpas I met!

After dinner, I went directly to the room where Adam and I were staying and lay there resting my weary legs and rubbing my Achilles tendons. Each room had a high-efficiency light bulb that was powered by a small hydroelectric generator nearby. Adam was able to unscrew the light bulb and tap into the electricity in order to charge our cameras and satellite phone. It worked out quite well, although we had to do without light while we were charging the equipment.

On the morning of May 2, after eating a hearty breakfast of eggs and Tibetan bread, we decided to leave our teahouse and walk around the village. There was a small stream that ran right through the centre of the village, down the side of the main pathway. The water from the stream was used to irrigate the crops of the locals, who either spent the summer there or lived there year round. It was also used for laundry, and we saw women washing clothes in different places throughout the village. In a few places, we could see the locals building additional teahouses, and we could hear the familiar "tap, tap, tap" rhythm of rock shaping that we had gotten so accustomed to in Namche.

After working our way partway through the village we found a makeshift wooden shack, inside of which the owners had installed two old billiard tables. The tables were extremely warped and in ill repair, but we decided to play a few games, and we ended up having a lot of fun — a welcome change from the long climbing routine.

We then made our way to a small building that we had learned had an Internet café. We sent a few emails and updated the blog that we had been maintaining for everyone at home to follow.

The Internet was painfully slow and cost twenty Nepalese rupees per minute, much more than in Namche, but it was the only option, and considering it was the highest Internet café in the world, we were quite happy to pay the price. We did try our best to bargain with the guy who ran the place, but he would not budge on his price. I guess he knew that he had a monopoly that high up on the mountain and that we would have to pay the price eventually.

Our second and third days in Dingboche we spent in a manner similar to the first. We ate, socialized, and played cards. We also went down to the billiard shack again and played pool with Jangbu, who had never played before. We emailed home once more, and thankfully we were even able to chat electronically with Natalie briefly over MSN.

We had been eating yak steak for dinner the three days we were in Dingboche, because it was about the tastiest thing on the menu.

When you ordered a yak steak at any of the teahouses, you could hear banging noises coming from the kitchen as they did their best to pound the tough yak meat until it was tender enough to serve. The pounding would go on for quite a while before they started cooking it. We often joked that the steaks must have been from old, worn-out yaks that they could no longer use for carrying equipment in and out of Base Camp. We never confirmed if this was true, and it was probably best that we didn't.

They always served the yak steaks covered in thick gravy, which made them edible and also hid what the steak actually looked like. It was not uncommon to discover after biting into them that the yak steaks were very stringy and tough, but at that altitude, they were tasty just the same.

After three days' rest and recovery in Dingboche, we decided that it was time to head back up to Base Camp. On the morning of our return, we woke up early and each of us had a cheese omelet with chips before starting back up the Khumbu Valley the same way we had come down.

Adam and I went on ahead of Dad and Laura, because Dad was still sick and very slow. The infection in his lungs was not getting any better. I was planning to stay the night in Lobuche or Gorak Shep, instead of going all the way to Base Camp, in order to minimize the risk of further damaging my knees or my Achilles tendons. However, I felt exceptionally strong that day, so Adam and I continued to push on past Gorak Shep all the way back up to Base Camp. It was a very long day, but it felt good to be able to go that kind of distance without any major problems.

Just before we entered Base Camp, two representatives from the Nepalese army stopped us and searched through our bags. Adam had not hidden our satellite phone very well in his bag, and they discovered it during the search.

Phones were one of the many items that were deemed prohibited to have at Base Camp, again because of the politics around the Chinese torch run. The phone was worth over US$750, and although we pretended that we did not know that we were not allowed to have the device, they confiscated it and told us that we could not get it back until three days later, after the Chinese reached the summit from the north side of the mountain.

This was quite a disappointment, because the phone was our only means of communication with home, and I thought for sure that we would not see it again once they determined its value. I figured they would sell it because it would generate more income for them at one time than the average Nepalese worker earns in a year. The average income was less than $500 per year, so items like that phone would be very valuable.

Up until that point, we had been very careful about hiding the phone and other items that were deemed prohibited. Arnold had suggested that nobody even mention the words "satellite phone" around the camp because there were liaison officers nearby, and you never knew who might be listening. Instead, he suggested everyone call the phones "pizzas." This code name is the term that everyone used during the expedition, and up until that point, we had not had any trouble.

Adam and I thought that Dad and Laura would spend a night in one of the villages below Base Camp because Dad was feeling so sick, but they decided to continue on all the way to Base Camp as well, and they arrived later in the day. It was good to be back at Base Camp because I knew that our push up the mountain was not far off, and I was eager to move on. I was able to fall asleep with no difficulty, because my body was again spent from the long trek. I knew that we would need at least two rest days before we would have recuperated enough to attempt another push up into high altitude.

17
Uneasiness at Base Camp

OUR TWO REST DAYS AT BASE CAMP WERE FILLED WITH much uneasiness and anticipation. Almost all of the Summit Climb climbers were at Base Camp for those two days, and tempers were high because the Chinese still had not made it to the summit with the Olympic torch, and thus climbing above Camp 2 was still prohibited.

Stories were spread around that likely had no truth to them at all, but people seemed to believe them. One story was that the Chinese had actually made it to the top but they were unable to light the torch while they were there and would have to try it again in a few days. Another story was that there was a big accident on the north side and the ambulance which was rushing the injured climbers down from the Tibetan Base Camp had driven off the road and flipped over. Still others were saying that the Chinese had already reached the summit but refused to let other people climb until they were off the mountain completely. Overall, it was very tense, and there was a lot of cursing and bad jokes made about the Chinese government.

Dad, Laura, Adam, and I were also restless but not nearly as bad as the other climbers because we had not been forced to wait around nearly as long — and because we had much better control over our emotions and tempers in general. Some climbers had been waiting at Base Camp or lower for a week or more, so some aggravation was to be expected.

I spent most of those two restless days reading, relaxing, and thinking about how nice it would be to be home and have things back to normal again. I wanted to spend time with Natalie, and I was dreading that she may have found someone else while I was gone. My mind conjured up all kinds of crazy scenarios while I lay in my tent, bored and frustrated.

The Khumbu Glacier, upon which the Base Camp tents were all erected, had moved and changed shape substantially while we were gone. The bottom of my tent, which had been reasonably level, was now sloped and uneven, with sharp rocks sticking up everywhere.

One nice surprise we received at that time was that Dan Mazur had sent up fold-out chairs with backs on them for the mess tent. This was an effort to brighten everyone's mood and to reduce the continuous whining and complaining that was going on. The simple stools that we had been using until then were quite uncomfortable and gave everyone a sore back, so the new chairs were much appreciated.

On the second night, I was quite cold and could hardly sleep at all. I still had the infamous Khumbu cough, which was probably coupled with a viral infection; I was coughing up all kinds of ugly stuff. My insides were still out of sorts as well, and I had to run to the outhouse tent on a regular basis. The explosive diarrhea, which we all seemed to get at times, would give about ten seconds' warning before one would need to find a place to squat.

We wandered around Base Camp and took some pictures with the Rotary Club flag, which Dad had brought, as well as my employer's company flag and Laura's school flag. We wanted to have some pictures to show in case we were not able to make it any farther.

We also walked to the bakery tent in Base Camp and bought

some pastries. The pastries smelled so good when we first entered the tent, and I thought the bakery was going to be a lifesaver and a taste of home, but the pastries turned out to smell much better than they tasted. But considering where we were and what they had to work with, they were marvellous, and visiting the bakery while in Base Camp became part of our regular routine.

Adam and I also decided that we would go back to the Nepalese army tent at the entrance to Base Camp to see if we could convince them to give us back our satellite phone. I did not really even expect it to still be there, but when we arrived, we discovered they still had it with them. I explained to the officer on duty that it was our only communication with our mother at home and that she would be worried sick if she didn't hear from us. It was true that it was our only way of communication, although I may have played it up a little to guilt him into giving the phone back. I guess he had a soft heart, because he returned the phone, and we gratefully received it.

As the Khumbu Glacier beneath Base Camp continued to melt, it created some artistic ice formations, including large rocks teetering on top of tall pinnacles of ice. There were also many birds arriving at Base Camp that were able to survive off the climbers' discarded food scraps.

At Base Camp, it was quite a challenge to hold back impatience or anger with the waiting, as we started to count the hours and minutes as they passed. It was extremely boring a lot of the time, and it was impossible not to miss all the things that were familiar and comfortable back home.

It required a heightened state of mental strength to maintain our composure over the seemingly endless time we spent acclimatizing and resting. We had to keep telling ourselves that we were not going to give up, no matter what happened, until we achieved our goal. This is very hard for people to do, which is one of the main reasons why fewer than 30 percent of the climbers are successful each year in reaching the summit. Most of the people who don't make it to the top turn around not because they cannot handle it physically but because they cannot handle it mentally.

Every day, you wake up and all you see is snow, ice, and rock. The sickness and the uncomfortable living conditions coupled with the strain on your body and the discomfort from the altitude sickness make it a very taxing environment to survive in. Eventually, no matter how much time, energy, and money climbers have put into their expedition, they talk themselves into going home.

I suppose we had been partially conditioned to handle that type of stress from the other adventures we had gotten ourselves into in life. Our mental strength came from a lifestyle of countless physical and mental adventures together as a family.

When I was in high school, we began competing in adventure races. In these team races, all three or four members of the team must navigate through the wilderness with a map and compass and find designated checkpoints, travelling mainly by foot, bicycle, and canoe. The most common races we competed in were eight-hour competitions, although we also entered multi-day races of two, three, or four days with either no sleep or short periods of sleep out in the wilderness.

These adventure races definitely helped in strengthening each of us both physically and mentally — elements that are a necessity for success on Mount Everest.

The first adventure race that we competed in was an eight-hour wilderness race in Parry Sound, Ontario, which wasn't far from our cottage; Dad, Adam, and I decided to enter as a team. There were eighty other teams competing, and as is typical for adventure races, none of the racers knew beforehand the details of the race start location or the route.

It was all new to us, and we felt a bit out of place, because most of the other teams had all kinds of specialized adventure racing clothes and equipment, and we just showed up in our shorts, t-shirts, and not much more than a few wooden paddles.

About an hour or so before the start of the race, we were given some topographic maps and a sheet with a set of six-digit grid references to plot the locations of the various checkpoints and transition stations onto the maps. The transition stations were where we would switch from one racing method to another (for example, mountain biking to canoeing or running to mountain biking) and the checkpoints were locations in the wilderness that we had to reach along the course of the race.

We weren't strangers to using topographic maps, so we plotted our coordinates and connected the dots to determine the bearings that we would need to set our compasses to in order to find each checkpoint. It wasn't as simple as plotting a straight line, though, because in between each of the checkpoints were often lakes, marshes, hills, rivers, cliffs, and many other challenging obstacles.

This is where strategy comes into play for adventure racing. From the topographic maps, we had to determine which way we thought would be best to circumvent all these obstacles in the shortest time possible.

Just before the start of the race, the organizers loaded all the teams into buses and drove us to a previously undisclosed location on an old forest road, where the race would begin. It was exciting to be starting in what seemed to be the middle of nowhere — a densely forested landscape with nothing but wilderness for miles around.

When the starting gun went off, about 250 racers, all in three-person teams, went charging into the forest, jumping over logs and dodging branches like a herd of frightened deer running from a predator. There were shouts and yells as some racers fell, got stuck in mud holes, or were separated from their teams.

Within the first few minutes, some teams started to break off in strange directions, while many of the others simply followed the leaders. It was very tempting to follow one of the teams ahead of us, but they didn't seem to be going in the direction we had set for ourselves, so before long, we veered off on our own course and soon were all by ourselves.

Checking the compass every few hundred yards, we continued running through the forest, although several times we had to wade our way through deep marshes or balance our way across logs and beaver dams.

When we finally came out of the forest to the first checkpoint at the end of a long hydro corridor, to our great surprise we were told we were the leading team at that point. Although we could see the other teams running along the hydro corridor not far behind us, that was all we needed to get our adrenaline pumping and light the competitive fire within us.

The rest of the race was an exciting adventure as we worked to increase or maintain our lead on the other teams. Our transitions between running, biking, and canoeing were rather slow, as it was our first time, but when we were moving, we felt filled with an intense drive to win, and we were racing at our full potential.

At times during the race, we were wading through mud with our mountain bikes held over our heads, and at other times, we were running while holding our canoe above our heads. But we were determined, and it paid off.

It was an incredible feeling to cross the finish line of our first-ever adventure race and be awarded first place. They even had a bottle of champagne for us, which was the icing on the cake!

After that first experience, we realized that we had found a sport that was perfectly suited to our lifestyle and interests, so we could hardly wait for the next one. We have since competed in many adventure races of varying difficulty and duration and have enjoyed them thoroughly.

18

Life at Camp 2

AT LONG LAST, OUR TWO DAYS OF RESTING AT BASE CAMP came to an end, and I found myself waking up before sunrise and preparing for another journey through the Khumbu Icefall. I made my way to the mess tent and started wearily forcing down some breakfast at 3:00 a.m.

We were supposed to leave at 4:00 a.m., but Adam and Dad were nowhere in sight, and our Sherpas had slept in as well, so we fell behind schedule. I waited around until 5:00 a.m., when Laura and Jangbu were finally ready. And then the three of us departed the camp ahead of Adam and Dad, who had just begun getting their things together. I was frustrated by their apparent lack of concern for the potential danger that they were putting us in by going through the icefall later in the day.

The icefall had changed a lot since the first time we had climbed through it. We could clearly see where there had been ice avalanches in places and the path had been rerouted to avoid the ice debris. Also, many of the ropes were stretched or broken from the opening up or closing of crevasses, and some of the ladders had been moved or were oriented differently. There seemed to be more overhanging seracs than the first time, and I remember trying to move quickly through the sections where they hung. It was difficult to do, though, because there were seracs everywhere, and I was not able to move very fast.

I pushed on ahead of the others to try to get through the entire icefall before the sun hit. I felt much stronger than I had during our first climb through, and I was only about 80 metres away from the final crest of the icefall when the sun's rays arrived.

We hadn't specifically planned beforehand to separate from each other on the climb, but often our physical conditions and unforeseen circumstances, such as sickness, made it complicated to always stay together. The distances between camps were so strenuous that I had to find the right balance between the energy I had to exert and the total time spent on my feet climbing. Climbing too fast would require far too much energy, but climbing too slowly was also very detrimental because it required carrying my pack for a greater period of time. For this reason, I would find a pace that was a comfortable balance and would be climbing in my own bubble for long periods of time before resting and regrouping with the others.

Even above the Khumbu Icefall, on the section of glacier below Camp 1, the route and ice formations had changed drastically. There were now very thin bridges of ice that we had to clamber across and a new crevasse to climb into that was narrow and deep and looked as though the walls would fall in at any moment.

Although I was moving much faster the second time through the icefall, it still took about seven hours to reach the tents of Camp 1. A couple of other climbers from the Summit Climb group were there lying on the ice, and I joined them for a while. The sun was very warm, and the winds were relatively calm by Camp 1 standards. I lay outside resting until Laura and Jangbu arrived and then eventually Dad, Adam, and Sangay.

The wind started to pick up again in the afternoon, and we all went into the tents and lit the EPIgas stoves to begin melting snow. The remainder of the day we spent in solitude, melting snow and eating soup, except for the few short times when we talked to each other over our family radios.

The following day, we continued up toward Camp 2. The hard part was that we had to carry much of the gear that we had brought through the icefall the first time as well as the gear we had just brought up the previous day. This meant that our packs were twice as heavy as normal, and it made crossing the ladders more difficult.

I started off by myself, and I could tell right away that I was going to have more of a challenge because of the extra weight on my back. However, I felt reasonably strong at first and made fairly good time as I trudged along the steep side of Mount Nuptse.

Adam, on the other hand, was not so lucky. He had caught a bad stomach bug and it hit him hard. He had intended to start off toward Camp 2, but he had to keep dropping his pants every few minutes to relieve his bowels. He had the horrible, explosive diarrhea that Laura and I had experienced.

Eventually, he was not quick enough fumbling with his zippers and ended up filling his drawers. I didn't find out until later because I had gone on ahead, but in his condition, Adam had no choice but to turn around and head back down.

As told by Adam Mallory:

On our second climb to Camp 1, I started out feeling good. I was tired from the early start, but by the time I met the rest of my family at the base of the Khumbu Icefall to put on our crampons and check over our equipment, I was looking forward to getting up the mountain. The plan was to climb to Camp 1, spend the night there, and then continue to Camp 2 the following day.

My climb through the icefall was faster than the first time, and I could tell that my body had acclimatized since last being there. The first indication I had that I was going to have a problem was after I had made it through the icefall and was climbing along on the less inclined area before Camp 1. Up until that point, I had been faster than Dad, but I was beginning to have to really work to keep up with him.

Upon arriving at Camp 1, I was quite tired and weak and went straight to one of the tents. The sun heating the tent had melted the snow beneath it, and the bottom of the tent was even more of a bowl shape than it had been the first time I was there. Initially the bowl shape looked quite comfortable, but it wasn't at all, and I kept sliding to the middle as I tried to rest.

The next day, I woke up and drank some water, and I could hear that the Sherpas were melting snow for making soup. My stomach started feeling a little funny, and I was dreading the thought of having to get up and climb to Camp 2.

One of our Sherpas, Jangbu, came by the tent a little while later with some noodle soup. The soup tasted good, and I ate the whole cupful and was even considering asking for more when I started to feel it. It wasn't long after I finished the soup that my insides started to hurt and I could feel my stomach churning. I had about one minute of warning, and I rushed to get my boots on and the tent open. I got to just behind the tent when the diarrhea hit me. I hadn't got my pants completely down either, and some had gotten on my pants. It was quite disgusting.

This was the beginning of my low point on the mountain. My diarrhea got steadily worse, and I started throwing up as well. At one point, I could no longer hold it in, and I just sat naked on the mat in my tent and cleaned myself up. Looking back, it was a very humiliating experience, but at the time I felt so sick that I didn't care who saw me.

Even the water I drank ended up coming right back up. I realized that I wasn't able to continue up the mountain and needed to get back down to Base Camp as soon as I could to recover. It was midday, and the rest of my family had already left and were continuing up the mountain when I, along with

Sangay, started to head back down.

As I left the camp, I felt so weak that I was worried whether I could even make it down to Base Camp. The climb down seemed to take forever, and every time there was any kind of rise in the rough terrain of the icefall, I had to stop and rest and would often throw up. It had taken us about seven hours to climb up the icefall that morning, and for me to go down it took over ten hours.

It was getting dark by the time we got to the bottom, and because of the sun's intense heat, a lot of the ice had melted and the rope anchors were just loosely sitting in the ice. I had to be very careful relying on the anchors in those instances. At one point, there was a small river that had been iced over on the way up but had melted and was now flowing. It was so dark by that point that we couldn't see a good crossing. We ended up jumping at a narrow area, but because of my weak state, I didn't make it completely across and ended up landing partly in the water and getting a wet foot.

When I got to Base Camp, one of the doctors gave me some pills, antacids, and electrolytes for my stomach. It took three full days for me to recover. I knew that during that time Dad, Alan, and Laura were climbing to Camp 3, acclimatizing their bodies to the higher elevation, and I was a little worried that that would be the end of my climb, as I would not have enough time to catch up to them. I was concerned that if I did climb with them, my body might not be sufficiently acclimatized and I would run the risk of getting severe altitude sickness.

On the fourth day after my return to Base Camp, I was well enough to try the mountain again. By that time, the others were coming down to recover, and I met with them only briefly before I headed up.

Climbing by myself wasn't much fun, and I had to be extra careful that nothing happened, as there was no one around to help me out. Due to my sickness, I had to fast-track my climb, and therefore I wasn't planning on coming back to Base Camp again before attempting the summit. I had to carry all the gear I would be needing for the remainder of the climb.

I had quite a heavy load, and I started to feel very fatigued after passing Camp 1. As I was getting closer to Camp 2, I radioed ahead, and Arnold, the team leader, came down to meet me and give me some support. The time seemed to crawl by while I was at Camp 2. I missed the rest of my family. I was by myself, the food was difficult to eat, and the environment was cold and miserable. I did some acclimatization climbs partway up the Lhotse Face and spent a lot of time just resting at Camp 2 and letting my body acclimatize.

———

At the time, I did not know anything about Adam's dilemmas, as I was continuing to slowly climb toward Camp 2. I had developed a bad headache from the altitude by the time I reached the camp, and I tried to drink water constantly so that the pain would go away, but it did not seem to work. It was nice to finally reach the camp, though, and I was greeted with a hot cup of lemon water brought to me by one of the other climbers.

I didn't have the energy to take off any of my equipment at first, so I just sat on one of the exposed rocks, sipping the hot liquid and warming my hands on the metal mug. I could not help but feel a little sense of accomplishment and relief. Another milestone had been accomplished; I had reached Camp 2.

Camp 2 was at an elevation of 21,300 feet (6,500 metres) and was situated quite close to the northern side of the Western Cwm. The camp was partially sheltered by the huge mountain wall that towered above it. There were enormous chunks of ice hanging ominously from the mountain wall, and I was concerned that one would break off and wipe out the tents.

The Summit Climb cluster of tents was at the lowest level of all the expedition tents at Camp 2, which were spread out fairly wide all along the edge of the Khumbu Glacier. Having the tents so close to the mountainside provided a certain amount of protection from the fierce winds and weather that were inevitable at that altitude.

The landscape, however, was far from ideal for laying out a camp. The terrain was made up of uneven ridges of ice and rock that had been pushed up by the glacier or had fallen from the steep mountainside above. There were also huge ice blocks scattered randomly around Camp 2, adding to the ruggedness of the terrain.

Shortly after arriving, finishing my cup of hot lemon liquid, and resting sprawled out on the icy, rock-covered surface beneath me, I decided to look around for a tent to sleep in. The Summit Climb group Sherpas had made multiple trips to Camp 2 in order to set up the tents, so there were approximately eight sleeping tents in addition to the cooking tent and a rustic dining tent.

News had come in that the Chinese were finally able to get the Olympic torch to the summit on May 8, which meant that the climbing restrictions had finally been lifted. However, this also meant that the other climbers who had been waiting around at Base Camp were all making a push up the mountain at the same time, and Camp 2 was very crowded. I believe that everyone from the Summit Climb group, except for Adam, was either at Camp 2 or was heading up to Camp 2 at that time.

I stumbled over to the nearest tent, which was quite close to the dining tent, and peered inside. The tent was perched on the side of the rocky slope, so only half of the tent was flat enough to sleep on. It was the tent farthest from the nearby towering seracs, and I remember thinking that if one of them broke off, I would have a better chance of survival from the location it was in.

In the centre of the tent was a large mound where the rock underneath had been forced upwards since the tent had originally been pitched there. Half of the tent dropped off steeply down the hill so that there was only a small space remaining, barely large enough for one person. There was also gear in the tent that had been left there by one of the other climbers on a previous acclimatization climb.

The general rule was that climbers could not reserve tents at Camp 2 or anywhere on the mountain, because there were not enough tents. They were claimed on a first-come, first-served basis as climbers arrived. I decided the tent I was inspecting was as good as I was going to get, so I threw my gear inside and moved the other gear that was left there into another one of the tents before starting to set up my sleeping bag.

Because of the shortage of tents, I knew that everyone would have to sleep two people to a tent and that Adam would most likely be bunking in the tent as well. I did not know at that time that Adam had not been able to continue up and had turned back to Base Camp. I realized that there would not be room for two people in the tent as it was and that we would have to move the tent to a flatter spot or lift the tent and adjust the rocks underneath. However, I was too exhausted to worry about that at the moment and thought that we would worry about fixing the unevenness of the tent when Adam arrived.

Eventually, Dad and Laura arrived at Camp 2 and came to my tent. They were equally exhausted and looked like they were almost at the point of collapsing. They told me that Adam had had to turn back because of sickness, and then they stumbled slowly up the slope to find themselves one of the last remaining tents.

There were times during the climb when one or more of us were so sick that we would separate the team for prolonged periods of time. This wasn't part of our original plan, and it certainly seemed negligent to leave one of our team members behind, but there really weren't any other viable options if we wanted to have a fighting chance at reaching the summit. The problem was that if the rest of the team waited for each of the sick climbers to recover, by the time the climber had recovered, another member of the team would more than likely have come down with a bad sickness as well, and the group would have to continue waiting for everyone to recover to no end. Each of us was stricken by severe sickness numerous times during the expedition and was forced to fall behind temporarily as the rest of the team continued with the climb.

The level of trust that we had developed as a team throughout the many other challenging endeavours and circumstances we had gone through together allowed us to make these decisions in the moment, without a lot of trepidation about the outcome. Not only were we comfortable relying on each other when we were together, but also we trusted each other to know what was best and right at the moment for ourselves. We had developed a level of interdependence that acknowledged self-sufficiency as a vital component of group strength, and at times we had to depend on that self-sufficiency.

I still had a bad headache from the increase in altitude, and I tried to drink as much water as I could while I rested in my tent. I did not go outside until dinnertime except when I needed to go to the washroom. Going to the washroom at Camp 2 was an experience. Taking a pee was fairly straightforward and only involved stumbling down the rocky slope a little bit so that I was downhill and away from the tents. However, every time the diarrhea hit me, which was quite often, I had to stumble out of the tent wearing my down boots, which had a smooth, rubbery bottom that provided zero traction, and down a long, icy pathway to the edge of a large wall of ice. The worst part was navigating around all the other partially snow-covered blobs of human waste that were strewn along the path.

There was no shelter or any place to sit. I simply had to lean up against the icy wall and try to avoid having my feet slip out from under me. It was indeed an experience in the freezing cold and not one that anyone would enjoy. Making my way back up the icy path was always a challenge as well, and I slipped many times along the way, once falling flat onto the ground.

At dinnertime, we got to experience our first meal in the Camp 2 dining tent. The dining tent was very primitive and basic. It consisted of a large, green canvas top and a few small rocks and crushed water containers for seats. It was quite uncomfortable eating there, but it was nice not to have to prepare our own meals.

There was no table in the dining tent. Instead, the drink mixes and jugs of hot water were balanced on a pile of rocks near the centre of the tent. There was a small cook tent next to the dining tent where one of the Sherpas prepared the food.

Around mealtimes, everyone would file into the dining tent and try to keep spirits high by making conversation. Sitting on the cold, jagged rocks or crushed water containers for long periods of time was very unpleasant, but that is what we had to work with.

Eventually, the cook would bring in a pot of food, and everyone would pass their plates down toward the cook to get them filled, hoping that they would not be coughed on too many times before they made it back.

Unfortunately, the food at Camp 2 was even worse than that at Base Camp. Almost every day, we had the Sherpa meal of dal bhat, consisting of rice and lentils. The altitude causes a person to lose his or her appetite, which made it that much harder to force down the dal bhat. Fried Spam was also a fairly common occurrence at Camp 2. I found the atmosphere and the smell of dal bhat hard to handle for any length of time, so I spent most of my time in my tent, reading and thinking.

One of the important things to look out for at Camp 2 was contaminated water. The problem was that all the water had to be generated by melting ice from around the camp, and because climbers had been using the Camp 2 area for years and it was located on a moving glacier, it was quite possible that the ice that we were using to make drinking water had been the location of a toilet spot in years past.

This was a disgusting thought, but it was reality, and all the water had to be boiled for a few minutes before it was consumed. It was hard to ensure that all of the water I drank had been properly boiled, though, because the Sherpas did a lot of the boiling, and there was no guarantee that they had boiled it for long enough. I tried to make sure I put iodine droplets in all my drinking water, even if it had been boiled, for that reason. There was a lot of illness at Camp 2, and many climbers were having to return to Base Camp to try to recover.

Since the climbing restrictions had been lifted, some Sherpas and climbers from the different climbing expeditions had started heading up the Lhotse Ice Face to set up Camp 3. We could see the climbers in the distance, looking like small dots slowly ascending the icy face. The Lhotse Ice Face is a 6,000-vertical-foot icy slope that begins at the upper edge of the Khumbu Glacier and slopes steeply up towards the sky at an angle of about forty degrees to seventy degrees in certain areas. Camp 3 was located halfway up the Lhotse Face at an elevation of 23,600 feet (7,200 metres).

We learned beforehand about the steepness and some of the dangers associated with the icy slope, but I remember thinking that it did not look that bad from where we were at Camp 2, a few kilometres away from the foot of the face.

By the evening of our first rest day at Camp 2, we learned that the Sherpas from our group had successfully reached Camp 3 and had set up a few tents on the steep slope. Although we had only just arrived the previous day, Dad, Laura, and I were planning to head partway up the Lhotse Face to get some experience on the steep incline and to expose our bodies to the higher altitude.

The excitement of exploring the unknown reminded me of the wilderness snowmobile trips that my father, brother, and I organize every year. We usually invite our friends and often some of our extended family along to take part, so generally we end up with a group of five to ten snowmobilers.

Our trips are always centred on exploring new areas and trying to reach remote locations where we haven't been before. We try to avoid any roads or existing snowmobile trails and instead choose to explore areas where we aren't likely to encounter anyone else along the way.

Using local topographic maps, compasses, and, in recent years, the GPS maps on our phones, we chart a path through the bush and usually try to follow marshes, ridges, or open areas as much as we can to avoid the dense areas of forest where some are sure to get their snowmobiles stuck in the deep snow. Pulling snowmobiles out of the snow is of course part of the adventure, but if it is a continuous occurrence, it can get very tiring.

Some years, the snow is over three feet deep, and it is quite a challenge to manoeuvre through the deep powder, especially in densely forested areas or climbing hills. The years with deep snow are the most enjoyable, though, because they offer a true challenge, and the feeling of carving and balancing a snowmobile through fresh snow is both exhilarating and in a way peaceful at the same time.

My favourite areas to explore are in the Canadian Shield, where there are high granite hills to climb, almost like small mountains. The act of zipping through the fresh snow while leaning the snowmobile to carve along the side of an open bedrock hill is a very enjoyable and exciting experience. The challenge, of course, is to see who can get to the top of the highest hills first, without getting the snowmobile stuck in the process.

19

First Time on the Lhotse Face

ON THE MORNING OF MAY 11, THIRTY-SIX DAYS INTO OUR climb, we all woke up quite early and headed over to the dining tent. We choked down a meagre breakfast as best we could. Spam and porridge had lost its appeal long ago, but we knew we needed the food for energy.

I remember being quite excited to finally step foot on the Lhotse Ice Face, which we had heard so much about. I got ready to go quite quickly and stood by the dining tent, waiting for Dad and Laura. I didn't bring a pack or anything extra — just water for the day and a few granola bars to keep up my energy. We were only going to be doing a short acclimatization climb on the Lhotse Face, and then we would be returning back to Camp 2. Dad and Laura decided to bring their climbing packs with them anyway so that they could have more of their gear with them.

As I mentioned earlier, the Summit Climb camp was the lowest camp at Camp 2, meaning it was farthest away from the Lhotse Face. I didn't realize how many tents were at Camp 2 until we started passing the other expedition tents along the way. Camp 2 was well spread out along the edge of the Western Cwm, and it was quite some time before we even got to the upper edge of the camp. Traversing alongside the expanse of

Camp 2 was relatively technical in itself, with steep, icy hills and rocky traverses along the way.

Eventually, we left the final tents of Camp 2 behind us and angled away from the edge of the glacier on a line toward the centre of the Lhotse Face. The glacier sloped up at a significant and ever-increasing angle all the way up to the start of the Lhotse Face. There were the usual crevasses to watch out for along the way, but none of them were anywhere near as large as those that we had encountered below Camp 2.

Dad and Laura were moving along quite slowly, so I went on ahead as usual, at my own pace. As I got nearer, the magnitude of the Lhotse Face became more and more apparent. It was an enormous expanse of ice, spread in front of me like a huge, white wall that angled up into the sky.

It was not possible to climb onto the face in most locations. This was because the uppermost section of the Khumbu Glacier had broken away from the Lhotse Face, leaving a deep crevasse between the two as well as a vertical ice wall. However, there was one section where a rib of ice protruded down from the Lhotse Face, and it was possible to cross there to begin the steep ascent.

I was in no hurry as I approached, and I stopped and rested for a while before putting on my climbing helmet. We had heard that ice and rocks often tumble down the Lhotse Face, so we had brought climbing helmets for protection against such projectiles.

At the upper part of the glacier, I arrived at the rib of ice. There was a fairly narrow crest that I had to cross in order to get onto the Lhotse Face and the fixed ropes began just before the crest to give climbers some safety while crossing.

Once I was at the base of the Lhotse Face, it became evident just how steep the ice wall in front of me actually was. I would estimate that the first section was at an angle of at least fifty degrees to the horizontal.

There were two lines of fixed rope heading up the icy face, one for ascending and one for descending, although a couple of climbers were ascending on each of the lines when I arrived. I noticed that the ice was very hard on the lower section of the face and that almost all of the snow had blown off, exposing the blue ice below.

As I approached the icy slope and prepared to clip into one of the ropes, I noticed that there was a constant stream of ice pellets raining down from higher up on the face. These ice pellets were mostly dislodged by other climbers above as they tried to secure their footing on the hard ice. The ice pellets made a unique rushing noise as they cascaded down the slope like a stream of small pebbles. Some of the ice chunks were quite large, and there were stones and rocks falling periodically as well. I figured that there was no point in waiting for the rush of ice pellets to taper off, as this was not likely to happen, so I clipped into one of the climbing lines and began kicking my way up the slope one step at a time.

I remember feeling quite precarious and vulnerable, hovering on the edge of the steep slope with only a few crampon points and a questionable climbing rope keeping me from sliding down into the gaping crevasse below. The shower of ice also made it difficult to keep an eye out for larger rocks and other objects coming from above, so I did not feel as though I was able to properly protect myself.

Several times my crampons slipped, and I slid a few feet before being able to stop myself. This was frightening. I knew it was not a good idea to rely at all on the fixed ropes because often the ropes and anchors could not be trusted. However, I found it almost impossible to climb without using the rope and thus used it almost continuously.

The other challenging part was the high number of climbers that were heading down the face, using the same rope as I was using to go up. Letting the downward climbers pass involved unclipping from the rope and supporting myself solely by my crampons. It was always a tense situation, and I remember distinctly when one of the climbers going down turned and bumped me with his pack as he went by. My heart jumped as I frantically tried to regain my balance and grasp for the rope above me. A fall would have resulted in serious injury or worse.

The pace was extremely slow, and it seemed to take an incredible amount of energy just to move my body up one small step at a time. Most of the time was spent just swaying back and forth, trying to catch my breath.

I decided to go up only a short way, to allow my body to experience the increased altitude and to get a feel for what the face was like. I did not want to tire my muscles more than I had to. I looked at my altitude watch at the point when I decided to turn around, and I was at 22,000 vertical feet. I had not made it very far up the Lhotse Face, but I decided that was enough.

Going down turned out to be even more nerve-wracking than going up. When I first turned my body around, I did not even know what to do with the rope at first to lower myself down. I began by falling a few feet and was barely able to stop myself by clenching onto the rope and ramming my crampons into the ice.

My legs were very shaky at first; it was a precarious situation to be in. I stumbled many times and swung sideways like a pendulum as I tried to steady myself. I definitely wasn't at a very good spot for experimenting with different ways to get back down, but I hadn't thought that far ahead and didn't have any other options.

What made it even more difficult than it should have been was the fact that the few climbers below me were pulling the rope very taut as they pulled themselves up. This made it impossible to wrap the rope around my body or my arms to use it as a brake as I descended.

Eventually, the rope slackened a bit, and I developed a technique that allowed me to inch my way down the ice. I wrapped the rope around my right arm in front of me and also grabbed the rope behind my back with my left arm. This allowed me to use the friction of the rope against my body to slowly lower myself down. Unfortunately, I relied on the questionable ropes and anchors the entire way back down. If one had broken, I would have been in serious trouble, but I did not see that I had any other choice.

After climbing back down onto the uppermost part of the Khumbu Glacier and getting far enough away from the Lhotse Face that I was confident I would not be hit by falling objects, I decided to stop and rest. I took off my pack and sprawled my body out on the ice. It was near noon hour by that time, and the sun above me felt quite hot. I lay there and waited for Laura and Dad to approach from below. Once they arrived, I told them about my experience and what they would be up against if they decided to give it a try. The three of us sat and talked for a while before they decided to continue up and try the Lhotse Face for themselves. I watched them leaving and took some pictures of them beginning to climb before I started back down toward Camp 2.

Laura and Dad had quite an interesting experience on the Lhotse Face themselves. Shortly after starting up the lower part of the face, they heard some climbers well above them shout, "Rock! Rock!" and before they knew it, a large rock came barrelling down to their left. They looked at each other as if to say, "That was close!" before they continued climbing. They hadn't made it very much farther when they heard climbers above them again yelling, "Rock! Rock!" What the climbers should have been yelling was, "Gigantic boulder!" because the second rock was enormous in size and came barrelling down again at a high speed, passing by them just to their right. Laura and Dad again looked at each other, and Dad remembers thinking, "First one on our left, then one on our right — the next one is likely to come directly at us."

A person has to be extremely careful and alert on the Lhotse Face to avoid these falling rocks and other objects. In 2007, a Sherpa was climbing on the lower section of the Lhotse Face when a large sheet of ice broke free and slid down toward him. He was not able to get out of the way, and the sheet of ice hit him in the upper body, decapitating him and taking his life.

Laura and Dad didn't go very far up the Lhotse Face either before returning as I had done after they had experienced its steepness and gained some altitude exposure. Dad was still feeling sick and was moving very slowly. It was quite a while before Laura and Dad returned to Camp 2, almost too exhausted to move. After we had been up on the Lhotse Face, the Camp 2 elevation did not seem nearly as high to our bodies as it had when we first arrived.

During dinner that evening, Arnold talked to us about the severity of pulmonary and cerebral edema. He also went over the drugs and injections we would need if we got either of these edemas further up on the mountain. As on the previous night, almost everyone in the Summit Climb group was at Camp 2, except for Adam, who was still at Base Camp recovering.

That night, we received a lot of snow, and the snow continued well into the morning. Some of the group's Sherpas left the camp to go down to Base Camp and bring up some more food. There was not much food at Camp 2 at that time, and many of the climbers were getting a bit upset about it because it meant that the only thing the Sherpas were able to feed us was the hard-to-stomach dal bhat. I rested most of the following day, alone in my tent. I was definitely sick and tired of the only surroundings we got to see — snow and ice. I longed for it all to be over so that we could finally go home and I could see Natalie again.

Dad crossing two ladders strung across a crevasse.

Crampon spikes locking onto ladder rungs.

Climbing out of a deep crack in the icefall.

A bad burn I got from the intense sun.

Vertical ladders haphazardly stacked together.

Starting to cross a thirty-five-foot-wide crevasse.

Vertical ice walls at the top of the Khumbu Icefall.

Laura grabbing onto the ladder hanging from above.

Crossing a crevasse on the Western Cwm.

Roped together with Dad on Mount McKinley.

Taking a closer look at a partially hidden crevasse on the Kahiltna Glacier.

Our tents in the Western Cwm at Camp 1.

Dad boiling maple sap in our large cast-iron cauldron.

Rappelling down a vertical ice face with Laura.

Dad displaying the melting that had occurred at Base Camp.

At the finish line of our first adventure race.

20

A Night to Remember

ON THE MORNING OF MAY 13, WE WOKE UP AND PREPARED to leave Camp 2 on our first climb up to Camp 3. The three of us started off together but soon separated.

Because of our late start, the sun was upon me long before I finished scaling the upper portion of the Khumbu Glacier. The moment the sun hit me and I was no longer in the shadow of the mountains around me, the temperature went from quite cold to very warm, and I had to take off my outer layers of clothing. Luckily, as I continued up the Western Cwm, some clouds moved in and some light snow began to fall, which reduced the heat and made it bearable. I finally arrived at the base of the Lhotse Face and was temporarily cast into shadow, because the sun had still not risen high enough to cast its rays onto the steep face itself.

I did not feel as awkward clipping into the ropes and starting my steep ascent up the lower part of the Lhotse Face as I had two days earlier. It was still almost as challenging, although I didn't have to deal as much with the showering of ice pellets that I had experienced on my previous encounter. Instead, there was a thin layer of snow sticking to the side of the icy face, which made it seem slightly safer and easier to gain a good footing.

I still had to rely a lot on the ropes and screw-type or

aluminum tee anchors that fastened the ropes to the ice. It seemed like the only way I could continue moving. It was far too difficult for me to ascend balancing and hoisting myself with only my legs.

It was an extremely slow process, and I felt I was hardly gaining any ground at all. Because of the small amount of available oxygen in the thin air, I could go up only one or two tiny steps before I would be forced to rest by either going down on my hands and knees or leaning back against the rope, gasping for air.

There were cracks in the ice of the Lhotse Face that I had to scramble over. There were also rounded protrusions of hard ice to cross along the way up. My whole body was exhausted in no time at all, and it took every ounce of energy I could muster to continue pulling and pushing my way up.

Eventually, after it seemed like I had been climbing for a decade on the steep, icy wall, I found myself gazing up at a slightly less inclined section where I could see a few tents in the distance. I was relieved that I had finally made some headway, although I was well aware that what I was seeing was only the lowermost cluster of tents and that our tents were in the uppermost cluster. The area around the tents was still quite steep, though it was not nearly as bad as what I had just ascended. I continued slowly pulling myself up, and eventually I arrived at the first cluster of tents, where I stopped for a much-needed rest.

There were a few other climbers in front of me and behind me, and they all looked as if they were in as bad shape as I was: hunched over, gasping for breath and then slowly staggering forward a few more inches at a time.

As I was resting there, I saw a climber above me who was clearly in distress. He was visibly suffering from cerebral edema, and likely some of the blood vessels in his brain had ruptured. As he approached me, I could see him staggering all over the place, and he looked like he was only partially aware of what was going on. He had a Sherpa with him who was trying to get him to lower altitude as fast as he could. His Sherpa had him by the arm and was trying to steer him in the right direction and pick him up every time he stumbled to the ground.

When the sick climber got to where I was resting, he staggered up to me and mumbled that he needed water. I had only a small amount of water left, but I decided to give him what I had, as he was in worse shape than I was, possibly at risk of losing his life if he didn't get down to a lower altitude very fast.

The decision I made at that point is a controversial decision among climbers and people in general. By giving up the only water I had with me, I was potentially putting myself at serious risk. Having enough water is crucially important for avoiding altitude sickness, and I did not know at that point how much farther I would have to climb.

The problem is that nowadays there are climbers who have the mentality that if something bad happens to them, there are other climbers there who will save them. There are so many sick people and others in need of aid on the mountain that if a person were to help every individual he saw who needed aid, there would be no chance of ever coming close to his end goal of reaching the summit, and he would very likely be putting his own life at risk every time.

The media has often cast a negative light on climbers who have walked past other climbers in need of aid instead of stopping to help them. I suppose I can see the validity of both viewpoints. On the one hand, there is the moral responsibility to do what is right which includes stopping and doing whatever one can to help another climber in need. On the other hand, there is the very clear likelihood that helping the sick person will result in your having to give up your own aspirations and possibly your own life. This also means giving up the years of training and preparation and the thousands or sometimes hundreds of thousands of dollars you have invested to make your dream possible.

Because of the narrow window of opportunity for a summit attempt as well as the extreme financial and time commitment involved, most climbers get only one chance to attempt the summit; to give it all up for an unprepared climber who shouldn't have been climbing in the first place is a complicated decision to make. The general way of thinking among most climbers is that you should be self-sufficient on the mountain and cannot rely on other climbers to come to your aid.

When I was climbing on Denali, I made a similar decision to help one of the other climbers who was too weak to carry some of his gear up to Basin Camp. I considered that I was carrying my own equipment anyway and I felt quite strong, so I decided that I would do what I felt was right. Dad had told me not to do it, and he did not take any of the climber's gear. Taking the extra weight meant I had to strain my legs, and this is what caused me to partially tear the Achilles tendons in both of my heels. Small decisions, even if made for honourable reasons, can have significant consequences. I was in an air cast for three months and could not run for three years, and I still have occasional pain in my Achilles tendons to this day.

I think it comes down to situational judgment. On the Lhotse Face, I knew the risk I was taking by giving away the last of my water supplies to the sick climber, but it was a risk I thought I could afford to take at that time. We must live (or die) with our decisions, whether they be good or bad.

There were a lot of anchored ropes around the lower cluster of tents that I could see on the Lhotse Face, although many of the ropes were old and frayed. A significant number of them were in place to tie down the tents so they would not blow off the Lhotse Face during a storm. There were also ropes connecting all of the tents together like a giant web. Those ropes, as we had learned from earlier research, were for safety. To prevent climbers from falling on the Lhotse Face, climbers should be clipped into the ropes at all times when they are outside of their tents or moving from one tent to another. This is because if you fall on the Lhotse Face at Camp 3, it is extremely difficult to break your fall, and you will more than likely fall all the way down the Lhotse Face, about 3,000 vertical feet, back toward Camp 2.

In the past, a few climbers have suffered this fate. Only a few years before we were there, a climber left his tent to take a pee wearing his down boots. He slipped, and before he or anyone could do anything to prevent it, he tumbled down the face and lost his life. Nobody has ever survived a fall on the Lhotse Face.

I looked behind me toward Camp 2, and I could see the clouds just below the camp in the distance. I could not see Dad or Laura because the Lhotse Face dropped off quite abruptly where I had just come up. It felt a bit surreal to be there, looking down at the high mountain peaks below me in the distance. The ice clinging to the sides of the surrounding mountains shimmered in the sunlight, and the majestic presence of the mountains was all around me. I paused just long enough to take it all in for a few moments and to try to fully appreciate where I was.

From the first cluster of tents, I had to ascend a very steep, nearly vertical, section of hard snow and ice. The section was quite taxing physically and took a long time to scale.

At the top of the steep ascent was the second cluster of tents. I was glad to see that the two clusters were fairly close together, and I had high hopes that the third cluster, including our tents, would not be far ahead.

I looked up past the second cluster at the vertical wall of ice that would be my next challenge. The subtle decrease in steepness at the place that I was at was because the section of ice that I was sitting on had broken off and slipped down the face a little way, leaving a vertical ice wall behind, known as a bergschrund.

The wall was not high, only about twenty feet in total, but I had so little energy that I knew it was going to be a challenge.

After a short rest, I forced myself to my feet and continued upward. When I arrived at the base of the vertical section, I stopped for a few minutes, leaning back and putting my weight against the rope while trying to find enough oxygen in the air to partially satisfy my lungs. Standing there, staggering at the base of the ice wall, I realized that it was larger than it had looked from a distance. In the weak state I was in, I knew it would take me a long time to ascend it.

Luckily, there was another climber ahead of me who was taking a long time on the wall and was only about halfway up by the time I had arrived. This gave me a few minutes to regain my clear state of mind and figure out a plan of how I should attack the ice wall in front of me.

There were two ropes dangling down from above, presumably one for climbing up and the other for rappelling down. While I was waiting, I saw a descending climber clip into the rope on my right and begin rappelling down the wall, so I decided that I should ascend the rope on the left as the climber ahead of me was doing.

Upon looking more closely at the hard, icy wall, I could see small crampon marks kicked into the ice. However, the small kick marks in the ice would not be sufficient for me to use as handholds; I would have to fully rely on the rope. I really disliked having to do this because there was no way for me know how well it was anchored at the top of the wall, and having seen the many poorly anchored ropes in other places along the climb, I didn't feel very secure or safe having to trust them. However, as with many of the other areas of the mountain, it did not seem that I had any other choice.

After the climber in front of me had reached the top and disappeared behind the upper lip of the icy wall, I staggered up to the wall and clipped my ascender onto the rope. I gave a few good yanks on the rope before proceeding, to give me some added peace of mind that the rope would break my fall if I needed it to. I looked behind me, and I could see that if the rope gave way, I would surely fall all the way down the Lhotse Face to my death. However, I had faced these types of situations before, and without further hesitation, I kicked one of my crampons into the first small ice divot I could see and started pulling myself up the ice, heavily relying upon the rope and my mechanical ascender.

Before I had gone very far, I became extremely short of breath and exhausted to the point of dizziness. My legs and arms began to quiver with the effort. I forced myself to continue moving, one small step after the next, until I finally was eye level with the top. It was a relief to see that the rope was anchored to two ice screws that looked very secure. I took a couple deep breaths, grabbed the cord which connected the two ice screws together, and heaved myself over the top onto the small ice ledge.

There were a couple of other climbers there preparing to go down, and they did not look happy that I had just rolled myself onto the small ledge at the top and was blocking their way as I gasped to catch my breath. Although I wanted to get out of their way, I could not move for about thirty seconds, and I must have been quite a sight as I lay there quivering and gasping.

The ledge I was on was not very large, and in front of me was a narrow crevasse about six or eight inches wide. It was nice to have the small ledge, though, which was in fact the top edge of the wall of ice. Beyond the small crevasse, the Lhotse Face continued steeply upwards.

Eventually, I staggered to my feet and moved toward the crevasse, leaning against the Lhotse Face so that the other two climbers could manoeuvre themselves and clip into the ropes to descend.

I peered back behind me over the edge of the ice cliff I had just come up to see if I could see Dad and Laura below me, but I could not. After resting a few minutes, I carried on, clipping into the next rope and staggering up the next section. It was quite steep in the area I was in, and it was very hard on my feet and ankles because of the sharp angle. The wind started to pick up, and I had to tighten my jacket around me to keep warm. The visibility decreased drastically, as well, from the blowing snow.

After thirty or forty minutes of climbing, I looked to my right and saw the remains of tents that had presumably been destroyed in a fierce windstorm. All that remained were a few anchors and some scraps of shredded fabric flapping in the wind. It looked a little disheartening and was a good reminder of the power of the storms. It was, however, reassuring for me to see, because I knew that I must be approaching the area where our tents would be.

It still took a very long time, though, before I finally was able to see some intact tents above me. There seemed to be two rows of tents off to my right, one higher than the other. The Lhotse Face was still extremely steep, even where the tents were, and I could see that the tents had been carved into the side of the face, in small cutouts in the ice. There were ropes leading off of the line I was clipped into and toward the tents and ropes connecting all of the tents together, as I had seen below.

I clipped into a rope that appeared to lead toward the upper row of tents, and I started traversing. The Summit Climb tents were a distance from the main rope that I had been following, and I was relieved when I saw their familiar yellow, which I recognized from the other camps. I stumbled over to the closest tent and let myself collapse on the ice in front of it. I looked at my watch when I finally arrived, and it had taken me seven full hours of climbing from the time I departed Camp 2 to make the ascent of almost 3,000 vertical feet. However, another milestone was complete. I had made it to Camp 3!

Five other Summit Climb members were already at the camp when I arrived. They had also made the push that same day and were planning on spending the night at Camp 3. Four tents had been set up there by our Sherpas, and I found out which tent was available and crawled inside.

The tent was very dirty: there were wrappers and food left in it by whoever had slept there previously. The worst part was that the sun's heating effect inside the tent had melted the snow below the tent so that the bottom of the tent had a very distinctive bowl shape to it, similar to my tent at Camp 1. I knew that I would have to accept the unevenness because I did not have the slightest bit of energy left to try to fix it.

Even when I had been resting in the tent for a while, I was still breathing very fast, almost hyperventilating, in order to get enough air into my lungs. I had a bad headache, and after I was able to melt some ice, I began drinking a lot of water so that I would minimize the likelihood of edema. I could hear the other climbers around me, and we made small talk by shouting between the tents. Christian, one of the Summit Climb support doctors, was using the emergency oxygen to help his body out. Christian had also brought a medical sensor which attached to a person's index finger to monitor vital signs. I wanted to know my heart rate and blood oxygen concentration, so I asked Christian if I could use it, and he passed it into my tent from theirs.

While I was lying in my tent, my resting heart rate was 120 beats per minute, and my blood oxygen was down to 67 percent. This was a concern because I had heard that most doctors consider anyone with a blood oxygen concentration below 70 percent to be in critical condition. It accounted for the fact that I could not seem to calm down my heavy breathing and racing heart. I returned the device to Christian and closed my eyes to try to get some rest. The sun's rays filtering through the tent made it quite warm inside in spite of the harsh conditions around me.

I pulled out my radio and called down to Dad and Laura to make sure they were all right. From Dad's reply, it was clear that he was in rough shape. They had just reached the vertical ice wall, which meant that they were moving extremely slowly and they still had a long way to go. It seemed unlikely that they would be able to make it all the way to Camp 3 because I knew how much distance still remained for them to climb.

After a while, I heard Jangbu arrive at the camp. I learned that he had gone on ahead of Dad and Laura with some of their gear. He told me that Dad was moving very slowly and that they would both likely need some help. After dropping some of the gear off and resting a bit, Jangbu left the camp and started back down the Lhotse Face to help them.

After about another hour, I could see Dad and Laura struggling toward the tents through the blowing snow. They were both on their last legs, and Jangbu was carrying Dad's pack. It had taken them ten and a half hours, but at long last they had made it. Dad looked very dizzy and wobbly when he finally reached the tents, and Laura was not much better. Dad probably should have used some of the emergency oxygen like Christian, but he would not.

I collected some chunks of ice from the ice wall above our tents, and Jangbu and I started two of the small gas stoves to begin the melting process. Laura and Dad did not have any energy to chip ice or do anything, really, so Jangbu and I generated drinking water for them as well. There was very little food at Camp 3, but we managed to find a few packages of noodles and some other dried soups. The warm soup seemed like quite a delicacy, considering the harsh conditions all around us.

We were quite exposed, perched precariously on the side of the Lhotse Face, and I could not help but think of the very real possibility that a chunk of ice or an avalanche could come down on us from above and we would not even see it coming. I tried to put these thoughts out of my head, though, because I knew they would not help the situation; we had no choice but to stay where we were.

Finally, well into the afternoon, the wind subsided along with the blowing snow so that visibility was restored. We were greeted by some pretty amazing views. It was truly awe-inspiring to be standing outside of the tent with my back to the Lhotse Face, looking out at the vast scene around me.

The steep, icy slopes of the Lhotse Face were on both sides, and the shiny ice glittered in the sunlight. Where I was standing among the tents, there was a huge bulge of ice on the face, creating the small, less-inclined area where the tents were able to be pitched. Farther to my right, though, the face was smooth and untouched except for a few rocks protruding here and there.

Looking out in front of me, I saw a blanket of clouds below us that looked almost surreal, covering Base Camp and the two camps below us. The huge slopes of Mount Nuptse were on my left, and the Everest Ridge was far to my right. These enormous ridges surrounded the cloud-covered Western Cwm where the Khumbu Glacier lay, although I could not see it beneath the clouds.

Mount Pumori could be seen right in front of us, poking up through the clouds beyond where Base Camp was located. Behind Mount Pumori, I could also see Mount Cho Oyu towering in the distance. We took some photos and short videos and enjoyed the warmth of the sun. It was an incredible view that not many people have the privilege of experiencing.

Although the views were breathtaking, it was not all fun and games. Being at 23,600 feet (7,200 metres) had its challenges. Because of the severely limited amount of available oxygen at Camp 3, it was very hard to do anything without gasping desperately for air. When I stumbled around between the tents or out to go to the washroom, the act of bending down to clip into the ropes seemed exhausting, and I really had to force myself to do it for safety.

I decided to bunk in the same tent as Jangbu, because that was where the stoves were kept, along with the little food that there was. The tent was quite congested with bags and other supplies, and it was uncomfortably set on the uneven ice beneath. The only Summit Climb tent that was available for Laura and Dad to use was the one I had been resting in earlier that had melted itself into a very deep bowl-shaped pit. It would have been impossible to sleep in that tent. There was, however, another tent right beside where Jangbu and I were sleeping which belonged to one of the other climbing groups. Since that tent was not being used and none of us had the energy to move or fix the Summit Climb tent, Laura and Dad decided to use it instead.

Most of the rest of the day was spent melting ice and resting our weary bodies. My heart rate did not slow down much no matter how much I tried to relax my body.

When the sun finally sank behind the mountains, I tried to get some sleep, but at over 23,000 vertical feet without supplemental oxygen, that was a challenging endeavour. The uneven floor of the tent, coupled with the lack of proper padding and the freezing temperatures, made it almost impossible.

My body slowly got colder as the night went on. In addition, because of the low oxygen levels, I experienced a fairly common altitude condition known as Cheyne-Stokes respiration, which has symptoms similar to sleep apnea. During the night, your respiration diminishes as you relax into sleep mode, but unfortunately this reduced breathing is not providing sufficient oxygen to your brain and other parts of your body, so you find yourself suddenly jolted awake, gasping for breath, as if you were drowning. After a night of this see-saw of falling asleep and jolting awake, gasping for air, and falling asleep again over and over, our level of exhaustion in the morning had hit a whole new level. We had to get down.

Although that first experience at Camp 3 took winter camping to an extreme, winter camping was not completely new to my family. In fact, for New Year's Eve of the new millennium, when the world was eagerly watching to see what disasters Y2K would bring, we decided to get away from it all and spend the night camping on a small remote mountain in Ontario known as Old Baldy.

We spent the majority of the day before New Year's snowmobiling through a blizzard and very deep snow to find our way to Old Baldy, and then we set up our tents on the top. I remember that Adam and I built a tunnel through the snow to the entrance of our tent and piled snow around the tent to try to insulate us as much as possible from the bitter cold.

At midnight, we were lucky that the wind died down and the skies cleared. Old Baldy is the highest point of land for miles around, so it was unique watching the thousands of fireworks exploding all around us from the many small towns way in the distance, many of them almost over the horizon.

We are not strangers to cold and bitter weather, and we often seek it out for such adventures. We have found that if we dress correctly for the weather with the right clothing and equipment, then the bitter winter is in fact very enjoyable.

These types of winter activities were very special for me, and I have many fond memories of the camaraderie and bonding that we shared on such family excursions.

21

Back Down to Recover

I WAS ALREADY AWAKE WHEN THE INSIDE OF THE TENT began to light up from the early rays of the rising sun. I was still completely spent and in a shivering state of drowsiness somewhere between asleep and awake, having had so little sleep during the night. The unevenness of the bottom of the tent had made it impossible for me to stretch out my body, and I had to try to sleep curled up in an uncomfortable ball. The entire night I had tossed and turned, and I felt utterly miserable. I asked Jangbu how he had slept; he had had a terrible sleep as well.

We got up out of our sleeping bags later than we had planned because of the cold, and immediately we started the routine of melting snow and ice for drinking water. I went out to see how Dad and Laura were. Neither of them had slept much either, as they, too, had suffered from the Cheyne-Stokes respiration and the other miseries that I had experienced all night.

I remember Dad saying that he was seeing stars that morning, as when one stands up too quickly, which was a serious concern, but there was nothing we could do other than get to a lower elevation. He was moving clumsily and stumbling around in a completely uncoordinated daze. Laura and I were not quite as bad, but the lack of sleep left us all feeling out of sorts and dizzy, making it all the more dangerous climbing on the side of the Lhotse Face.

After we had packed up all our gear and put on our crampons, we turned our backs on Camp 3 and began climbing across the Lhotse Face toward the route we had come up. Dad, Laura, and I took our time getting to the ropes because, in addition to the stresses of a bad night, our bodies were in bad shape from the exertion the previous day.

I felt Dad was being quite irrational and making some silly moves, but it was hard for any of us to think clearly and act rationally. When we arrived at the ropes, Dad was still seeing stars, so I showed him the best way to clip into the ropes to rappel down the Lhotse Face. We hadn't really practised rappelling much up to that point, which was a mistake, because Dad had almost forgotten how to do it. The first time he tried to lower himself down, he caught a crampon, stumbled, and fell quite a few feet with his heavy pack on his back before he was able to get himself stopped. He was rushing things and was very easily aggravated. Luckily, though, he managed to get the rope skills back fairly quickly, and we all started down the icy face.

On the really steep sections, I used my figure-eight rappel device, but most of the time, I would just wrap the rope around my arms and my body to slow my descent. Before long, I was able to perfect this method, and by running the rope behind my back and twisting it around my left arm, I was able to apply a fairly controlled braking pressure against the rope when I needed it. I always made sure that I had a carabiner from my harness clipped onto the rope just in case.

It was much more manageable going down the Lhotse Face than it had been climbing up, although even going down was exhausting. After a few hours of clipping in and out of the ropes and lowering ourselves down the various steep slopes, we reached the bottom, and I left Dad and Laura to go on ahead to Camp 2.

It was a relief to get back to Camp 2. I had some warm drinks right away and some noodle soup to replenish my liquids. When Dad and Laura arrived back at Camp 2, Dad said he wanted to continue on back down to Base Camp. I was skeptical, because it looked as if he could hardly walk, and I did not like the idea of going through the icefall once the sun was upon it. However, given the value of getting into the more oxygen-rich area of Base Camp, it made sense to keep going down.

I wanted to get through the icefall before it had a chance to really warm up; I packed as quickly as I could so that I could get started. Dad decided he should try to get some sleep or at least some rest for about an hour before he continued, but Laura decided she would head down right away along with me. After we had strapped on all of our gear once more, we headed off together.

It was about 11:30 in the morning when we turned our backs on Camp 2. The heat from the sun was penetrating and it was fiercely bright climbing through the Western Cwm with the sun's rays reflecting off the snow-covered mountains on both sides. We removed our coats and as much of the warm clothing as we could, but it was still very intense as we trudged along with our packs on our backs, wearing our large, high-elevation glacier boots.

When we got to the icefall and rappelled down into it, the temperature was equally scorching, and we could feel the ice soft and slushy beneath our feet. We made very good time. I pushed on as fast as I could to get through in the shortest amount of time, and Laura kept up the pace well.

During the descent, there were several avalanches falling from the steep side of the Lho La pass, noisily rushing down the mountain walls into the outer edges of the icefall. From Base Camp, we had seen large avalanches from Lho La come thundering down, bringing a mountainside of snow that would spread across the icefall and cover the climbing route in a plume of snow and ice. We could only hope that we would not encounter an avalanche of that magnitude while we were there.

The route through the icefall had once again changed due to the movement of the glacier. Near the bottom there were small pools of water collecting between the ice ridges, and the pools were slowly draining, creating many creeks and small rivers as the water cut its way through the ice.

Just before the bottom, a large waterway had formed perpendicular to the route. It had a ladder across it because there didn't appear to be any way to get around. I remember thinking how unfortunate it would be if I were to stumble and fall off into that frigid water.

I had started developing a stomach ache shortly after we began descending through the icefall, and as we continued down, my stomach problems got worse. I was in a lot of pain when Laura and I arrived at Base Camp, and the discomfort was to the point where I was clutching at my stomach to try to relieve the pain.

We met up with Adam, who had been recovering at Base Camp the entire time we had been up at Camps 2 and 3. He filled us in on what he had been dealing with, and we outlined all of the challenges we had faced during our adventure to Camp 3.

After only a short time at the camp, my stomach pain had worsened to the point that I was running to the latrine quite frequently to vomit. I didn't really have any food in me, so it was mostly dry heaves over and over again until I thought I would throw up my insides. With my insides churning and aching, I had to repeat my dry heaving routine at least once every hour for the rest of the day and evening.

I got some medication to ease my discomfort, but by the time I was ready to go to sleep, the pain was so severe I could not really keep down any of the medicine. I was severely dehydrated as I lay in my tent but could not drink any water because

I didn't want to throw it up, which would happen immediately when I did. I felt awful that night and could not get any sleep for hours because my stomach and body hurt so much. Every way I lay caused me pain and acute nausea. I remember my body quivering from the sickness and exhaustion I was experiencing.

Eventually, I was able to find a position that seemed bearable to my stomach. I lay on my right side, and as long as I didn't move at all, I thought I might be able to get some sleep. I longed for sleep to come over me to take the misery away. Eventually and thankfully, the relaxing blanket of sleep took over.

In the morning, I woke up feeling significantly better. I was able to drink some water, which my body desperately needed. This was a welcome relief because dehydration is the enemy of climbers at high altitude. After talking with a few of the other climbers, we agreed that my problem was most likely caused from a gas pressure buildup in my intestines and stomach. I am not entirely sure if this is what it was, but I know it was quite a relief to be rid of the intense pain.

Adam left Base Camp at 4:00 a.m. that morning to head up to Camp 2. He had fully recovered from his sickness by that point and was eager to make up for the time he had lost and catch up to our climbing schedule. I was able to eat breakfast, although I did it very cautiously, half-expecting to have to run out to the latrine as I had done the night before. Mostly, though, I just continued to drink liquids. My stomach had still not fully recovered, and I did not want to return to my prior state.

We borrowed a solar charger to charge our satellite phone, and we gave Mom a brief phone call after it was charged to give her an update of where we were and note that we were still alive. Mom was quite lonely and having an emotionally difficult time at home without her family. She was very glad to hear from us and know that we were all right.

There were noticeably more avalanches all around Base

Camp than there had been earlier in the expedition. This was because the days were getting warmer and the ice and snow was becoming softer. Laura and I both had bad sunburns on our faces, and Laura had a very bad burn on her neck that was making her skin bubble and was very painful for her.

My wrists were also burnt where they had been exposed the previous day, and my tongue was burnt as well, making it hard to taste anything (which wasn't necessarily a bad thing at that point). My muscles were also awfully sore, having not fully recovered from the long climb down from Camp 3.

The next four days were spent resting at Base Camp to recover our strength, trying to cure ourselves from our sicknesses, and waiting for Adam to complete his acclimatization on the Lhotse Face.

To try to minimize the boredom, we went to visit "Loco," our Vietnamese friend whom we had met in Namche. We also went to the bakery almost every one of those four rest days. The days seemed to drag on forever as we waited for the hours to slowly pass.

I was able to use the shower tent, which felt so good, but with the tiny amount of water that was available in the plastic pump container, it just made me miss being able to have a real shower at home.

At one point during those rest days, I decided to make a Spanish crossword puzzle for Dad and Laura to do. I had been studying Spanish on and off for a few years by that point, and I thought it would be a productive thing for me to do to help pass the time. Laura and Dad both also had studied Spanish, and it gave us a reason to put our minds to use.

On May 17, one of the other climbers at Base Camp had a scary experience that almost claimed his life. Our team doctor, Christian, was sitting in his tent reading when one of the gigantic boulders adjacent to his tent slid down on top of the tent, crushing half of it. It landed right where his head would have been if he had been lying down at the time. He was very fortunate that he was sitting upright, or he would have been killed by the huge rock. A lot of rocks were shifting and rolling around Base Camp at that time because the ice was melting rapidly.

We received word via the radios that Adam had completed his acclimatization climb partway up the Lhotse Face. This was good news because it meant that he would be returning to Camp 2 for a few rest days, and we would be able to start back up the mountain to meet him there before the four of us continued on to attempt what we hoped would be our final push up the mountain.

On May 18, Loco came over to our tents with a group of other climbers from the Vietnamese team. We talked for a while, and he was telling us about a doctor from India who was at Base Camp with a group of climbers he was supporting. The doctor had given Loco's group a lot of help, and Loco suggested we go to see him. My throat had been sore for a long period of time and didn't seem to be getting any better, so I thought it was a good idea. Laura also wanted some relief from the bubbling sunburn on her neck, so she wanted to get him to look at that. And Dad had his share of ailments as well, so we headed off with Loco to the Indian doctor.

Dr. Burfal was his name, and he was a pleasant, mild-mannered man. We shared some good laughs in his group's tent before he decided to have a look at us. After looking at my throat, he gave me some Indian medicated syrup. I was grateful, and the syrup worked quite well after I had taken it for a few days.

Dr. Burfal helped out climbers at Base Camp by diagnosing and giving away a lot of medicine. He was a very kind-hearted man. The Himalayan Rescue Association, we heard, did not think much of him, though, because they have outposts at a lower elevation where they get paid to diagnose and give out medicine, and he was doing it all for free. He had a quick look at Laura's neck and told us that we should come back the following day and he would give us a full checkup.

We decided to accept his offer, and the following day after breakfast, we returned to his tent. He checked our blood pressure and other vitals and then gave us some medicines that we might require. He disagreed with the medicine Christian had given us for pulmonary and cerebral edemas and gave us some other medicine instead. We didn't know which medicine would be the best, but we decided to keep both just in case.

The day before our scheduled departure finally arrived, we set about packing all our gear and preparing for the following day's climb. The thought of going back up was appealing, although I was very anxious about the state of the icefall, which was far more dangerous in the warmer weather with the ice melting. I was quite pleased that my throat pain had subsided thanks to Dr. Burfal's syrup, but I had begun to develop quite an upset stomach, which filled me with dread that my prior abdominal condition may be returning.

22

Leaving for the Final Push

ON THE MORNING OF MAY 21, I AWOKE QUITE EARLY, FILLED
with mixed emotions. On one hand, I realized that I was not
fully recovered, and the thought of having to force my way up
the Khumbu Icefall, Western Cwm, and Lhotse Face and then
into the unknown above Camp 3 didn't seem like a good idea.
On the other hand, though, after having spent so much time on
the mountain, I was anxious and excited to be starting our final
push to the top.

We again left late, and it was already light by the time we
reached the beginning of the icefall. I stayed with Dad and
Laura through the icefall to take some photos of them, and we
stuck together until we had scaled the final ice wall, and then I
went ahead on my own.

I stopped by Camp 1 to have a quick snack that I had brought
along and then moved on quite slowly. My legs were already
completely exhausted by that time, so it was a challenge to
push on even at the snail's pace I was going.

Not long after I had passed Camp 1, a fierce blizzard arrived
and the snow began to accumulate. I was in the cloud layer
as well at that point, so the visibility was poor, and I was able
to see only a short distance in any direction. Eventually, my
exhausted legs could not hold me up any longer, so I lay down

beside one of the thin bamboo markers that were marking the route in that particular area. After ten minutes of rest, curled up in a ball, I forced myself to push on.

I looked ahead and could just make out two bamboo markers a short distance ahead. I tried not to think of how far I had to go, because it was still a great distance, and my body was spent. Instead, I forced myself to get to the second bamboo marker, and then I collapsed again for another ten minutes. I continued this routine, bamboo marker after bamboo marker, in order to inch my way up toward Camp 2. It took forever, and it seemed like I was never going to make it.

The distances that I was able to cover between bamboo markers got shorter and shorter as time went by, until finally I saw the outline of Camp 2 in the distance. I was completely drained by the time I reached the tents, but I was glad that my technique had worked and I had finally arrived.

I have used that technique of focusing on smaller steps instead of a seemingly impossible goal many times during my life in order to keep moving in the direction I want to go. It is an excellent method and one that I highly recommend for anyone who is serious about reaching their goals in life. Splitting goals into short-term, manageable segments is the key to achieving long-term success.

Adam had set up his climbing gear in the tent that I had used the previous time at Camp 2, and there were some empty tents, so I decided to move the gear that I had left there into one of the other tents. I piled my stuff into a vacant tent, crawled inside, and collapsed.

Laura and Dad had been having a terrible time getting to the camp as well, and they were still a long way back. They called us on the radio to say that one of us would have to go back to help them.

Laura was very sick and was vomiting frequently along the way. The gastrointestinal sickness she had caught had become quite serious and was causing her internal bleeding to the point where there was blood showing up in her vomit and diarrhea. She was in desperate need of medical attention as she was continuing slowly upward.

I could barely move my body, but Adam had been resting at Camp 2 waiting for us and had energy, so he decided to go down and help. When he met up with them, he took Laura's pack from her and gave them much-needed encouragement to push them forward. This was one example of how working together as a family gave us a distinct advantage that individual climbers who joined a random climbing group would not have had.

I fell asleep fully dressed shortly after I had collapsed in my tent. It was early afternoon at that point, and I did not wake up until after dinner. This meant that I did not get any food or water in me, which was not a good idea. I knew that I had made a mistake by falling asleep without hydrating, so I drank down some liquids and had a small snack before going back to sleep again.

The following day, we woke up to snow falling, and it snowed for the entire day. Laura said that she thought she felt a little better, but I felt a lot worse, and I was sure that I had caught whatever sickness she had. I was having to run to the washroom area numerous times throughout the day. Eventually, I decided to take two Imodium pills to stun my bowels because I couldn't be running down the slippery path every five minutes. I also took a ciprofloxacin pill to try to kill whatever bugs were inside of me.

The blizzard that we were experiencing was not in the weather report that we had received from Base Camp. It was difficult to predict the weather on the mountain because it can change so suddenly and the big mountains effectively create their own weather. Surprise storms are not uncommon, and climbers have to be prepared for anything.

At dinner on May 22, we discussed our climbing strategy

again. Laura said that she didn't think she would be able to climb the following day, and we all wanted to attempt the summit together, so we pushed our summit attempt back by one additional day.

I couldn't bear the thought of eating any more dal bhat in the dining tent, so I got some hot water and made a freeze-dried meal in my tent.

We got news on the radio the next morning about the weather forecast for the next few days. We also got some sad news that a climber had just died around Camp 4. The thought of this death left me a bit numb, knowing that we would be following in the footsteps of the deceased climber.

That extra day at Camp 2 waiting for Laura to recover seemed like a long day. I tried to fill the time by doing things like fitting and adjusting my oxygen mask, which we would soon begin using, along with my goggles. They did not fit very well together because the oxygen mask came so high on my face, but I was able to play around with it until I got a configuration that I thought would be sufficient. I also took one of my balaclavas and cut a hole in it to make it work with the mask. As the sun went down, the excitement and anticipation built inside me for our departure in the morning.

On the morning of May 24, we awoke early, dressed quickly, loaded our gear in our packs, and headed out of Camp 2 toward the Lhotse Face.

Laura was still feeling sick and weak, and she fell behind early on. Adam and Dad were also moving slowly, so I went on ahead. I was feeling more comfortable and relaxed on the Lhotse Face, since by that time in the expedition, we had spent many hours on its steep slopes. I was able to move slightly faster than before, but it was still an extremely long and excruciating process fighting my way up.

The sun was out and it was warm for the first half of the ascent, and I remember thinking to myself, "I wish I did not have this bulky, down-filled mountaineering jacket on me!" It was just getting in the way and causing me to overheat. That kind of thinking was an example of the mentality that causes a lot of climbers to perish or lose body parts to the cold. The weather can be so pleasant when the sun is out that some climbers leave camp with only a light jacket or light mitts. The weather on Everest can change quite suddenly, and I found that out first-hand.

I had just reached the base of the first vertical section on the face when, within minutes, a storm came in from the far side and I was in a complete whiteout. The temperature went from quite warm to frigid cold in an unbelievably short period of time. The wind was howling and the snow was whipping in every direction. I was forced to zip my mountaineering jacket all the way up and tighten the hood drawstring to bring the thick, down-filled hood around my face so that I basically had no skin exposed to the elements. It was incredible how cold and miserable the weather became.

After I had adjusted my jacket, I pushed on through the storm, up the vertical sections, and a few hours later, I stumbled into Camp 3. Once I had rolled my mountaineering pack into one of the tents, I found an ice axe and started chopping some pieces of ice off the nearby ice wall. I then lit one of the camp stoves to melt the ice while I waited for the others. Before too long, Dad, Adam, and Laura arrived, and we sorted out the sleeping arrangements. It was amazing how much better we felt just from the acclimatization we had achieved since our last climb to Camp 3.

There wasn't much food left at Camp 3, but we managed to find some powdered soup packages and had some hot soup and granola bars.

Adam and I stayed in one tent, Dad and Laura in another, and Jangbu and Sangay in a third. In order to reduce weight for our summit attempt, Adam and I had brought only one thick, down-filled sleeping bag for the both of us. For the summit attempt, we had planned to sleep wearing our full down-filled pants and jackets and unzip the one sleeping bag to drape over us. This is a common practice for climbers on the summit attempt, because it is necessary to carry as little weight as possible. Adam and I had agreed to alternate each day, one carrying the sleeping bag and one the sleeping mats.

We found each of us an oxygen cylinder, which we had planned to use for sleeping that night. It is recommended to sleep using a small amount of oxygen at Camp 3 because it saves energy that will be needed for higher up.

Adam and I hooked our oxygen cylinders up to our masks, and it felt good to have the extra oxygen boost. We tried to fall asleep with the masks on, but it was a challenge. Adam kept knocking his mask off in his sleep, which was a concern because knocking your mask off higher up while sleeping can be dangerous or even fatal. I woke Adam the first time I noticed that his mask had fallen off so that he could put it back on.

I had a difficult time falling asleep at all with the mask on. If I was lying on my back, moisture from my breath would condense and build up inside the mask and then subsequently drip down onto my face, which was very unpleasant. Even when I was on my side, it gave me a lot of problems, so eventually I just turned my oxygen cylinder off, got rid of the mask, and fell asleep without the oxygen.

I had a much better sleep than the first time that we had slept at Camp 3, but I woke up early just the same. My body was more acclimatized by that point and did not have to work quite as hard to survive on the low available oxygen at that altitude.

The morning was cold and crisp, the winds were calm, and there was no sign of bad weather. Dad slept in and took a long time to get ready to depart. After waiting for a while, Adam and I decided to go on ahead. Jangbu followed suit shortly after we left and caught up with us as we were adjusting our oxygen masks at the edge of the camp.

The route beyond Camp 3 continued steeply up the Lhotse Face, so right off the bat we were struggling our way up an icy slope, one step at a time. I developed a bit of a rhythm with my climbing where I would take two small steps upward and then count for five seconds while I took deep breaths to try to get some oxygen into my deprived lungs before taking two small steps again.

The oxygen system that we were using was a continuous flow system, meaning that instead of being on demand, the oxygen slowly and continuously seeped into our masks, partially enriching the air we were breathing. We used a very low amount of oxygen at that point, just enough to preserve our energy for higher up.

Even at a higher flow rate, the enrichment was nowhere close to the oxygen concentration available at sea level, but it was enough to make our bodies feel as though we were at an altitude of approximately 2,000 feet lower than we actually were. Thus, by using supplemental oxygen at the summit of Everest, our lungs would receive the same level of oxygen that is present at 27,000 feet, even though we would actually be at just over 29,000 feet.

It was an excruciatingly slow process inching our way up, and every little movement we made was exhausting and required rest to recover.

After a few hours of climbing, Adam and I reached a point where the route turned and cut across the Lhotse Face. Although traversing the face was not quite as taxing as it had been going steeply up, it was still a very slow process, and we had to make sure we were clipped into the safety ropes at all times because the face dropped off steeply to our left. One wrong move could result in a tumble to our death if we had nothing to stop our fall.

As we traversed the face, we were heading toward a band

of yellowish-brown rock called the Yellow Band. The route across the Lhotse Face was angled upwards toward the Yellow Band, and the size of the band became more apparent as we approached. What had seemed like a small, colourful pattern from a distance was in fact quite a large, jagged obstacle for us to scale. Adam and I decided to wait for Dad and Laura before starting to climb it.

The first part of the Yellow Band was the most difficult. We had to climb up a near-vertical section of jagged rock and snow before the ascent became slightly less inclined. Although the vertical section was only about twenty feet high, it seemed to take forever for us to claw our way to the top. At sea level, the climb would have been quite easy, but clinging to the rocks and ropes at that altitude took a huge amount of energy, and I was gasping for breath the entire way up.

What should have taken less than a minute with normal oxygen levels took us each ten to fifteen minutes, and when I finally heaved myself up the last portion of vertical rock, I had to lie on my side for about thirty seconds, gasping for air, before I was able to crawl out of the way.

After the first vertical rock climb on the Yellow Band, there were more ledges to climb up, but most of them were small enough that they could be overcome with short bursts of energy.

When I finally reached and surpassed the last portion of rock on the Yellow Band, I was faced with a seemingly straight-forward snowfield to cross. Compared to the steep climbing we had been doing that morning, the snowfield almost looked flat from my vantage point at the top of the Yellow Band. The route angled across what could be considered the uppermost portion of the Lhotse Face.

My movements were exceedingly slow, and it seemed to take a huge amount of energy just to unclip my carabiner and clip it into the next rope at each of the anchor points. I spent more time stationary and trying to catch my breath than actually taking steps forward.

Before long, I broke away from the others and went on ahead at my own very slow but steady climbing pace. There were other climbers out that day, some going up the snowfield and some heading down. I had a few close calls passing by the climbers who were traversing down.

There was not a lot of room to manoeuvre, and one of the passing climbers must completely unhook from the safety rope in order for the climbers to pass each other by. For some reason, I was usually the climber that unhooked, and a few times the other climber's pack would hit me and throw me off balance. I can remember one instance very clearly where the other climber turned and their pack struck me and knocked me backwards. Luckily, I was able to grab frantically for the rope, which saved me, but the occurrence gave me a real fright.

Although the snowfield had looked fairly easy at first glance, it turned out to be inclined fairly steeply upwards, and it took what seemed like forever to cross. Hour after hour, one foot in front of the other, I trudged on, and the next landmark, the Geneva Spur, never seemed to get any closer.

I looked behind me when I had reached about the halfway point of the snowfield and saw that Adam had fallen back — presumably to wait for Dad or Laura — but Jangbu had passed him and was pushing on ahead of the others to catch up with me.

I had to put myself in an almost hypnotic, low-energy state in which I didn't think about anything else except religiously putting more and more of the snowfield behind me as I inched my way toward the base of the Geneva Spur.

The Geneva Spur, like the Yellow Band, had seemed fairly small from a distance, but as I neared the base of it, it began to tower above me like an ominous wall of unforgiving, jagged black rock.

Eventually, I reached the first rocky outcrop of the Geneva Spur, where there were a few other climbers resting. I dropped myself down behind the rocky outcrop and rested for about fifteen minutes. Jangbu had been slowly gaining on me, and after ten minutes or so, he arrived at the rocky outcrop and plunked himself down beside me.

The Geneva Spur was a difficult section of the climb for a few reasons. Due to its steep jaggedness and the fact that it towers above the snowfields around it, the wind had blown most of the snow off of the side of the Geneva Spur that was facing us. The sharp crampons that we were wearing on our mountaineering boots work very well on ice and snow but not well on exposed rock. The metallic spikes slip. For this reason, I took my crampons off for climbing the Geneva Spur but even the hard plastic of my mountaineering boots slid quite easily on the rock, and I had to be very careful about my footing.

Another challenge of the Geneva Spur was that nobody took down any of the old ropes. Presumably this was because nobody has the energy or willpower to do so at that altitude. This meant that there were a lot of old, tattered ropes on the face of the Geneva Spur, and it was difficult to know whether the rope we were holding onto was the current year's rope or if it was one that had been degrading in the sun for many years, in which case it could break under our weight at any time. Our only real solution for this problem was to hold onto or clip into three or four ropes at a time. We thought that surely one of them would be strong enough to hold us.

To further complicate that particular section of the climb, the uppermost section of the spur was nearly vertical, and it was quite a challenge to clamber up the exposed rock in such an oxygen-deprived environment.

I sat there with Jangbu, assessing the route up the spur, and in spite of the challenges, I was not overly concerned. Compared to what we had gone through already on the mountain, I considered the Geneva Spur a controllable and calculable challenge to overcome. Jangbu and I forced ourselves to get up and keep moving.

As I started climbing, my boots slipped repeatedly, and I had to rely on the ropes and my hands gripping the rocks to break my fall. The steep section near the top was especially nerve-wracking because, as I glanced behind me while hoisting myself up the jagged rock, it was apparent that a fall from there would certainly be fatal. The sharp rocks of the Geneva Spur below me terminated at the edge of the upper part of the Lhotse Face, which dropped off to oblivion.

It was a great feeling to roll myself over the uppermost rock ledge. I had made it up the Yellow Band and the Geneva Spur and was now almost at Camp 4. I lay at the top for a while, resting and taking in the scenery around me.

The surrounding panorama was absolutely incredible. I was now so high up that I could see overtop of most of the soaring mountains that surrounded Base Camp and made up the Himalayan range. The mountains, which stood in rows in front of me one after another, almost seemed surreal from my vantage point. Amidst the hardships and difficulties I had experienced up to that point in the climb, gazing out at the wonder in front of me as I rested was pure bliss. I was fortunate enough to be experiencing what most of the world can only dream of and was filled with awe at the majestic landscape surrounding me. The efforts of mountaineering are extreme, but the rewards can be limitless.

After resting a few minutes, I again forced myself up to continue on. The route followed along the top of the spur and was relatively flat leading up to Camp 4. I trudged along slowly and was in no hurry because I did not want to waste any energy unnecessarily. Adam, Dad, and Laura were quite a distance behind, and I did not see any reason to arrive especially early.

Other than the lack of oxygen, the wind on the top of the

Geneva Spur was the only real difficulty. It was quite intense as it howled across the top of the spur. I was blown partially off of the trail a few times and had to hold on to the ropes to keep from falling sideways on other occasions. Eventually, the wind-whipped tents of Camp 4 came into view, set on the barren, exposed rock of the South Col, the saddle-like area between two peaks.

23
High Camp

THERE WERE NOT MANY TENTS AT CAMP 4 COMPARED TO the other camps; there were only about ten in sight. The tents that were there were taking quite a beating from the fierce wind, which was tossing them back and forth, almost tearing them apart with every gust.

Up until that point in the climb, we had seen very little garbage and debris along the route. There had been a strong effort in recent years to clean up the mountain and everyone was doing a great job, which resulted in the mountain seeming pretty clean overall. At Camp 4, however, there was much more debris. At such an extremely high altitude, it is so difficult to move that nobody has the energy or willpower to take even an extra ounce along with them when they are descending. They are often just trying to get out of their with their lives, and many don't, so they leave whatever they don't immediately need.

The debris was mostly shreds of old tents that had been destroyed sometime in the past, pieces of old rope still fastened to the rock, and some food remnants and packaging that were left behind by other climbers. The place looked like a desolate island of rock among a sea of towering peaks. The strong, steady winds basically never subsided at Camp 4, constantly battering the tents and any climbers who were outside.

It made us feel very vulnerable in our silent thoughts about what we would face next.

Camp 4 is the High Camp, meaning that it is the last camp before the summit, and it is in the area known as the "Death Zone." The Death Zone is the area above 26,000 feet (8,000 metres), where there is not enough oxygen to support life. As long as a person stays in the Death Zone, their body's cells continue to die, and no new ones are being made to replace them; if a person stays more than a few days at that altitude, they run the risk of not even having enough energy to go back down.

Death is a real occurrence in the Death Zone, and I could not help but have this in the back of my mind, even though I tried to suppress the thought as much as possible. Almost every year, a few people perish around Camp 4, and the year we were there was not an exception. Three climbers had died already by that point.

In general, the deaths are of climbers who are older or who have climbed too fast and not paid attention to the early signs of acute mountain sickness. However, there are deaths from unavoidable causes as well, such as avalanches and unpredictable weather. I felt that we had climbed at a slow enough pace that we weren't at very high risk of acute mountain sickness. However, I was still feeling sick from a bug that I could not get rid of, Dad and Adam were not much better, and Laura was the sickest of us all.

It is quite an eye opener and a sobering experience when you hear of people losing their lives doing the same climb that you are doing and at the same time you are doing it. It is not the same as reading it in the newspaper or seeing it on television. When the news of another dead climber came in, it was real and immediate, giving me an uneasy feeling.

We learned that it is often climbers from poorer countries around the world who perish on Everest. Some of the poorer countries send or sponsor climbers to attempt Everest for prestige reasons — for instance, if they have never had a citizen make it to the summit. The problem is that the climbers often have so much pressure on them to succeed that they will make mistakes in judgment at critical times and lose their lives in consequence. If they make it to the top and get back down alive, they return home a national hero, their families are taken care of, and they live a good life. But if they come home unsuccessful, they have to go back to the same terrible living conditions that they left.

This knowledge often drives them to keep going no matter what happens and causes them to climb too fast and take undue risks. They are scared that they will miss their opportunity or the weather window to make it to the top, so they rush their climb and end up getting an edema and perishing.

My family has been touched by the death of climbing friends. We had two close friends from Ohio who died in a tragic climbing accident. Dad and Adam had first met twin brothers Jerry and Terry climbing Mount Aconcagua in South America. After beginning the climb, Jerry and Terry realized they had forgotten a piece to their climbing stove which would have prevented them from being able to climb, but luckily Dad had an extra of that very part, and he was able to lend it to them. They were able to continue the climb and successfully reached the summit together. We became good friends with them after that encounter.

They were very good-natured, fun-loving, adventurous people, and for this reason we enjoyed spending time with them. Jerry and Terry used to come up to go snowmobiling and exploring at our cottage, and we visited them at Terry's home in Ohio as well.

When Dad and I decided to attempt to climb Denali in 2004, we determined that we would climb along with Jerry, Terry, and Jerry's son Jeremy. We had a spectacular climb with them, and four of us made it to the summit, but Terry unfortunately felt too weak to make the final push to the top.

One year later, in 2005, Terry and Jerry returned to Alaska for another attempt so that Terry could make it to the top as well. They both had reached the summit, and on the descent, on a very steep section called the Denali Pass, they both fell, tumbled down the steep slope, and lost their lives.

It was tragic news, and when we heard of the accident, we drove down and attended their funeral in Ohio. Their passing gave us a shocking reminder that life is fragile. Mountain climbing can be a dangerous endeavour, and the risks and safety measures should not be taken lightly.

On the Christmas before Terry's death, he had sent us a framed poem that he said he tried to live by. I have included it here because the message is meaningful, and it is our memory of him. The original poem, "The Guy in the Glass" by Dale Wimbrow, is a little different, but this is how Terry knew it:

The Man in the Glass

When you get what you want in your struggle for self
And the world makes you king for a day
Just go to a mirror and look at yourself
And see what that man has to say.

For it isn't your father or mother or wife
Whose judgment upon you must pass
The fellow whose verdict counts most in your life
Is the one staring back from the glass.

Some people may think you a straight-shootin' chum
And call you a wonderful guy,
But the man in the glass says you're only a bum
If you can't look him straight in the eye.

He's the fellow to please, never mind all the rest,
For he's with you clear up to the end,
And you've passed your most dangerous, difficult test
If the man in the glass is your friend.

You may fool the whole world down the pathway of years
And get pats on your back as you pass,
But your final reward will be heartaches and tears
If you've cheated the man in the glass.

When I arrived at Camp 4, I could not find our Summit Climb tents and soon became frustrated, stumbling around trying to locate them. I had already wasted a lot of energy walking around the area where the tents were at least twice when Jangbu arrived and brought me to the correct location.

Three Summit Climb tents had been pitched at Camp 4. Jangbu threw his pack into one of the tents, and I stumbled over to one of the others to do the same. However, when I zipped the tent open and attempted to climb in, I discovered that there was another climber sleeping in the tent. He was not part of the Summit Climb group but had climbed to Camp 4 relying on there being an empty tent for him to squat in. With the help of Jangbu, I was able to get him to leave the tent so that I could get things organized before Adam arrived. More than likely, the other climber that we had ousted simply wandered around until he found another empty tent belonging to one of the other climbing outfitters.

From talking with the other climbers later, I learned that this was a fairly common practice for some of the poorly organized or unsupported climbing groups or individuals. There were enough tents around that they relied on there being at least one empty tent. In this way, they didn't have to worry about bringing a heavy tent, and I imagine they were almost always able to find one available.

The third tent at Camp 4 was occupied by one of the other Summit Climb members, Linda, and her personal climbing Sherpa.

It was a welcome relief when I crawled into the tent and zipped it up most of the way closed, allowing the lower half of my legs with boots and crampons to remain outside. I did not have the energy to take off my crampons at first, so I just lay there on my back for a period of time, trying to relax. It felt like such a liberation to be inside and free of the relentless howling winds, and I felt like I was finally able to gain some control of myself and of the chaos that seemed to be all around me.

I kept my mask on and the oxygen flowing, although I turned the regulator down to a lower setting to conserve oxygen, as I was no longer moving and my body would not be needing as much. My heart rate still did not slow down much, pounding in my chest at an elevated rate, a constant reminder of the physiological strain that I was putting on my body. I was not in any hurry to move. I was well ahead of Dad, Adam, and Laura, and I didn't really have anything pressing to do, so I took advantage of the time just to rest for a few minutes.

Eventually, I summoned up the energy to take off my crampons and to start unpacking my sleeping gear. It had been decided that Adam and I would share a tent at Camp 4, as we had done at Camp 3. Similar to Camp 3, we would continue to sleep in our high-altitude clothing with a small roll-up mat under each of us to separate ourselves from the cold rock and ice below us.

About half an hour after I had finished setting up the tent, Dad arrived at Camp 4. I could hear him stumbling over to where the Summit Climb tents were, and he sounded almost delirious with fatigue.

He stumbled over to the tent where Jangbu and Sangay were and collapsed inside. Adam arrived some time later, slumped into our tent, and helped me finish setting up. After a while, we thought we should check on Dad. We went over to the other tent, and Dad replied in a murmur that he was okay but he wanted to make sure Laura had some warm noodles ready for her when she arrived. He didn't have the energy to do anything at that point, so Adam and I started taking the necessary steps to make Laura the warm water.

We found a partially frozen trickle of water that was created by the sun's heating up the black rock in one location. We were able to get some water from the trickle, although it was a slow process. Once we had collected a few Nalgene containers full of water, we returned to the tent and set up the stove to start boiling the water.

After a considerable amount of time, Laura finally arrived at the camp. She was moving at a snail's pace and was completely exhausted, as Dad had been when he arrived. We decided that Laura would have to stay in the tent that Adam and I were in, as there was no room for her anywhere else.

We helped Laura get out of her crampons and boots and managed to find some room for her to squeeze into the tent. She ate the noodles we had made for her but did not have the energy to do anything else.

Adam and I ate some dried granola bars in the afternoon, which I suppose would be considered our lunch and our dinner, since we did not have anything more to eat that day. There was supposed to have been some food brought up and left in the tents for the summit attempt, but this was either overlooked or, more likely, taken and consumed by another climber.

As Laura did not arrive at Camp 4 until quite late in the afternoon, it meant we had only a few hours to prepare and ready ourselves; before we knew it, we would have to leave on our summit attempt.

Climbers usually leave late in the evening of the day that they arrive at Camp 4 and climb throughout the night. There are two reasons for this. First, the weather is often a little better during the night. But more important, it generally takes at least twelve hours to get from Camp 4 to the summit if one is fit and acclimatized, and it is preferable to arrive at the summit during daylight. It can take much longer if climbers are weak or sick. The rule of thumb is that if you have not reached the summit by noon the following day, then you need to turn back, no matter how close you are. A large number of the deaths on Everest are of climbers who refused to turn back at noon and instead continued marching on to their own demise, eventually running out of oxygen and not having enough energy to get back down.

For the few hours that we had at Camp 4, Dad was completely exhausted and just lay in the tent in the position in which he had collapsed. He was able to get some much-needed rest, which was essential because he would not have been able to continue in the state he was in when he arrived. Laura and Adam also were lying down in our tent in a state somewhere between resting and sleeping. As I was the only one able and willing to move at that point, I headed out to get us more drinking water. It was essential that we get some water for the climb that we had ahead of us that night, since there would not be time later.

It was already late in the evening at that point, and it had become very cold. The wind was as strong as ever, beating the tents with relentless force and giving no indication that it would let up.

Unfortunately, with the temperature drop, the little trickle of water that Adam and I had found earlier was completely frozen. I used the bottom of the Nalgene bottle to try to break some of the frozen ice crystals, and I was able to collect a decent amount of ice from the frozen trickle. I wasn't able to get enough, though, and I decided to walk far away from the tents, where I was able to find some snow that I thought might not have been contaminated.

The snow that I was able to find was very hard, almost like ice, and I again had to chip away at it in order to be able to collect it. It took a long time for me to collect enough, and my hands were nearly frozen by the time I turned back toward the tents.

The sun was no longer visible, and the light was fading by the time I got back. Before going into the tent, I stopped for a minute to look up at the towering South Face of Mount Everest, which I knew we would be attempting to climb in a few short hours. It was both exciting and terrifying to think about it. The South Face looked almost impassable because of its steepness. It appeared to go up forever at a near-vertical angle. Jangbu had pointed out to me the small plateau known as the Balcony at the top of the South Face. It was impossible to determine the exact location of the route, though, and I did not ponder it for very long before heading back into the tent with the snow I had gathered.

Adam and Laura were attempting sleep when I returned. There was hardly room for all three of us and the boots and gear as I attempted to settle myself inside the tent. After I zipped up the outer flap of the tent's vestibule, Adam woke up, and we started melting the ice and snow that I had brought.

By the time I shut off the stove, it was around six in the evening. We had decided to leave at seven, which meant there was really no time for me to sleep or even rest. I lay down and tried to make the best of the next forty-five minutes but was not able to sleep at all. At 6:45, I sat back up in the tent to get ready to depart.

I woke the others as well so that they could start preparing to leave. It was almost completely dark at that point, and I was eager to get going. I got ready quite quickly, but none of the others bothered, unfortunately, so I was the only one ready to depart at the time that we had agreed upon.

I was admittedly quite angry about this, as I could have gotten some more rest if I had known that this would be the case. I stood outside waiting for an hour and a half. And at 8:30, on the night of May 25, we departed on our attempt to reach the summit.

24

The Final Ascent

EACH OF US WAS FULLY DRESSED IN OUR DOWN-FILLED outerwear and all the other warm clothing we had brought. We brought our climbing packs, but they were almost completely empty except for two oxygen tanks each, our water supply, a few energy bars, and a few articles that we planned to leave at the top. We were all wearing our oxygen masks as we headed out, and I must admit it felt a bit crazy to be heading out on a twelve-hour climb at that time of night. It was pitch black, and all we had was our small headlamps to guide us toward the South Face and, ultimately, toward the summit.

Before long, we left the rocky area around Camp 4 and were travelling across the fairly flat glaciated section at the base of the South Face. I was very sluggish, and it took a while for my body to accept that I was forcing it to keep climbing, even though I had given it no sleep and basically no rest. The fairly flat icy section did not last long, and before we knew it, the terrain beneath our feet began to angle upwards. It began to snow before long as well, further reducing the small distance we were able to see in front of us with our headlamps.

We had gotten partially separated from each other, and although we were not that spread out, the reduced visibility made it seem that we were much farther apart than we actually were. Dad and I were ahead of the rest, slowly marching on at what seemed like a snail's pace, but it was as fast as we could force our bodies to go.

Before we had been climbing for an hour, we got a call from Laura on the radio. She had still been feeling very sick that morning from the illness that was causing her the internal bleeding, and she was still very weak and slow moving. She called us to say that she had soiled herself and had a fall from which she was unable to get up from for several minutes due to lack of energy. She said that she would be unable to go on and would have to head back to the tents at Camp 4. Dad wanted to make certain she was sure of her decision and would be okay to return to Camp 4. She sounded heartbroken to be heading back, but in her situation she did not really have much of a choice. We said goodbye to Laura over the radio, and as she turned back toward Camp 4, the three of us continued on upwards with our two Sherpas.

Separating from each other at that altitude in the pitch black of night may not have been the wisest decision in retrospect, but our diminished mental capacity at the time did not allow for a high degree of rational thought.

As the route continued to get steeper, we found that there were fixed ropes that had been installed by other climbing teams in the past, and we were able to clip into these ropes for safety. The danger again was that, as on the Geneva Spur, many of the ropes were old and tattered, having been installed many years before. The incline just continued to get steeper until we were going up a very steep slope of about sixty degrees to the horizontal. It was a slow and tedious process as we simply tried not to think, just concentrating on putting one foot in front of the other and ignoring our surroundings.

The weather continued to get worse as we climbed. The snow became more intense, and before long, we were in a blizzard with the wind blowing the snow fiercely across the South

Face. My goggles had long since filled with ice because of the fact that they didn't fit well with the oxygen mask; my breath would enter the goggles, fog the lens, and then freeze on the inside of the lens. I had been taking them off every few minutes to scrape the ice away, but eventually it was too hard to see, and I opted to go on without wearing the goggles. Climbing without goggles can be dangerous; many climbers have frozen their eyeballs. I made sure that I kept my hood up and that the wind was not blowing directly into my eyes.

Eventually, rocky outcrops began to appear in front of us on the steep slope, and we had to slowly and painfully scramble over these rocky sections. Many of the rocks stuck out of the South Face, and in order to climb over them, we had to pull ourselves up the small vertical sections of rock.

This was exhausting, as we slid on the rocks while working hard to prevent a fall. It was also quite dangerous because we were relying on the fixed ropes to pull ourselves up. Not being able to see the anchors or the state of the ropes above made it a precarious situation, but we did not have the energy to get up the ledges without the aid of the ropes. I would often give the rope a hard tug before I put my weight on it. This definitely wasn't a reliable safety test, but it gave me a bit of peace of mind.

At that point in the night, my mind was very sleepy, and the lack of oxygen was really affecting my thought process. I felt like I was operating in a dream world, functioning with only a portion of my usual mental capacity. Unfortunately, it wasn't a particularly good dream. It was frigid cold, tedious, and exhausting.

The blizzard continued to escalate as we pushed on and I had gotten quite a distance ahead of Adam and Dad. I could just barely see Dad's headlamp behind me as a dim glow flickering through the blowing snow, and at times I could not see it at all.

Separating ourselves as we did on that steep section of the

South Face wasn't necessarily a bad idea, as it was important that each of us try to be at least one anchor point apart so that we did not have two people pulling on the same anchor. Also, it was very hard for the upper climber to make use of the rope if someone was pulling on it from below. The pulling force held the rope taut against the rocks and ice, rendering it difficult to get a hold of. As well, it was quite painful for the upper climber if they had the rope wrapped around their hand for grip and the climber behind put their full body weight on it.

Although the weather and terrain was extremely harsh and quite unpleasant, the worst part by far of that climb through the night was the malfunctioning of my Jumar ascender.

The Jumar ascenders that we were using were designed to slide freely when pushed upward on the rope but to grip firmly onto the rope when pulled in the other direction. To accomplish this, there was a small, spring-loaded cam with many sharp teeth on it. These teeth were angled so that they released when pushed up the rope but dug into the rope when moved in the other direction.

The problem was that the blowing snow would coat the outside of the ropes in a layer of snow crystals, and these crystals would build up on the teeth of the cam. Eventually, the ice was thick enough that it completely covered the teeth. When this happened and I pulled against the rope, to lift myself over a ledge, for example, the ascender would release and I would slide backwards. I often fell quite a ways down the mountain before I was able to stop myself by grasping frantically at the rocks, snow, and pieces of rope with my gloved hands. It was terrifying whenever that happened.

The only way to rectify the problem was to unclip the Jumar from the rope, take my mitt off, and scrape away at the ice with my fingernail until some of the teeth were again exposed. This was very tedious, and my hand would go numb to the point where I would have to put it inside my jacket to keep it from freezing. I had to go through the process of scraping the teeth countless times in order to keep moving upwards.

Adam and Dad also experienced this problem. Dad was especially frustrated by the frightening recurrence. With the snow and the cold and all the other problems we already had to deal with, he recalls it being the only time during the climb that he thought, "If this mountain throws anything else at me, I may have no choice but to turn back."

After six long hours of very steep and gruelling climbing, I finally arrived at the small plateau known as the Balcony. I arrived before the others and stopped to rest on the ice in front of a large, rocky outcrop.

There were several empty oxygen cylinders left near the rocky outcrop, as this was the spot where most climbers stop to rest and change their oxygen bottles. I was so tired at that point that I could hardly keep my eyes open. Lying on the ice with my eyes closed, I hovered at the point between sleeping and waking, trying not to let myself drift off. When the others reached the Balcony, they sat down and rested for a few minutes as well.

I can't remember specifically, but I'm sure I must have fallen asleep during those few minutes, as Jangbu had to shake me to bring me back to reality. We didn't allow ourselves to spend more than ten or fifteen minutes at that spot before we prepared to go on. Our oxygen cylinders were almost empty, so we removed them and stowed them with the rest of the bottles by the rock, and after connecting our full oxygen bottles, we again forced ourselves to our feet and pushed on.

As we were leaving the Balcony and heading up the Southeast Ridge, the sleep deprivation hit me the worst. I had rested on the Balcony, and I guess my body had started to shut down. It was about 2:30 a.m., and I hadn't slept in over eighteen hours.

As I staggered away from the Balcony, I could hardly keep

my eyes open. My eyes kept rolling backwards, and I felt like I was swaying all over the mountainous ridge. This sensation of being in a sleeping state as I walked lasted for a few long and tedious hours. The slope at that point was less steep than the South Face had been, and although the Southeast Ridge was a fairly sharp-edged ridge, I was clipped into the fixed ropes most of the time, so I just let my mind shut down as much as I could while I trudged along.

Around 4:00 a.m., the first rays of the morning sun began to peek through the clouds below us on the distant horizon, and it was a glorious sight. We had made it through the night. This helped energize our spirits, awakening us to some incredible scenery as the surrounding panorama emerged with the new light.

We were at a point well above all the surrounding Himalayan mountains, and the view was breathtaking. We could see for miles in every direction all around us. In places, there were patches of cloud, but for the most part, the weather was clear and in our favour.

The angle of the sun cast a large shadow of Everest on the surrounding mountains, a reminder of just how huge and majestic the mountain truly was. The clean, white brilliance of the mountainous peaks was contrasted by the darker valleys in between. It felt almost like looking down from the heavens from that altitude at the lesser peaks below. It was a beautiful sight.

The Southeast Ridge began to get quite steep as we trudged along. Many times during that section of the ridge, Jangbu and I would go on ahead and then sit and wait for the others to catch up. Eventually, the ridge turned into a rocky, near-vertical face, with many old and a few newer-looking ropes anchored haphazardly in various locations along the way. The rocky face went up for a long way, and we could not see the top when we started to scale it.

Scaling that rocky area was an extremely slow process. We

Dining tent and sleeping tents at Camp 2.

Inside the dining tent with Dad at Camp 2.

Enjoying some fresh snow with Dad and Adam.

Dad heading off toward the Lhotse Face.

Resting near the base of the Lhotse Face with Dad and Laura.

Climbing up a steep incline on the Lhotse Face.

View down at the clouds from Camp 3.

Laura in front of tents at Camp 3.

Laura very sick near Camp 2.

Leaving Camp 3 wearing our oxygen masks.

The Yellow Band from a distance.

Adam climbing on the Geneva Spur.

View from the top of the Geneva Spur of the surrounding Himalayas.

Camp 4: High Camp.

Looking up at Everest from Camp 4.

Dad at night with his headlamp.

basically clawed our way up, inch by inch, stopping countless times to gasp for enough oxygen to continue.

It was quite a technical climb, especially in the exhausted and weak states we were all in. It was also very frustrating because our metal crampons kept slipping on the hard rock. As we had done previously on the mountain, we tried to clip into as many of the questionable ropes as possible, just in case any of them failed.

The rocky face seemed to go on forever, but eventually I dragged myself over the last of the rocks and onto another small, icy plateau. We had reached what is known as the South Summit.

The view from the South Summit was also breathtaking. The South Summit sticks up above the ridges on both sides of it, so it feels like you have reached the top when you arrive. This is why it is often also referred to as the "False Summit."

We stood for a bit on the South Summit to regain our composure and to study the section ahead of us. It was like a tug-of-war. On one hand, after we had worked so hard to get to that point, the ultimate goal, the summit, was almost in sight. On the other hand, we could see a cloud plume drifting off at an angle near the top, representative of very strong winds. Would we be blown off the narrow, treacherous spine before even reaching the summit, and would we be able to return if we did reach the summit? It required a lot of willpower to suppress the cold wave of fear.

We were faced with a very jagged and tricky looking ridge separating us from the summit. The Summit Ridge looked treacherous and unforgiving, with a steep drop of about 2,000 vertical feet on both sides.

We knew that we had no choice but to continue if we wanted to reach our end goal. We looked at our oxygen pressure gauges, and we each had ten MPa of oxygen in our cylinders. After consulting with our Sherpas, we decided that this would be enough oxygen to get us to the summit and back down to where we were on the South Summit; we later found out that this was a costly error of judgment. We stowed our spare oxygen cylinders there on the South Summit, planning to pick them up on the way back down.

Before getting onto the treacherous ridge, we had to go down about ten or fifteen feet on the far side of the South Summit. From that point on, the climbing got very difficult right away. There were sections of jagged, inclined boulders that we had to clamber over, with crampons constantly slipping on the exposed rock. The route ran just to the west side of the crest of the Summit Ridge, and for most of the way, there was a steep buildup of ice on our right-hand side.

One of the larger boulders that I can recall was like an inclined plateau, and I had to crawl across it on my belly, grasping the shreds of rope that were hanging there, tattered and blowing in the wind.

The last of the large rock climbs is known as the Hillary Step, named after Sir Edmund Hillary himself. The Hillary Step is a near-vertical wall of rock about forty feet high that represents the last serious obstacle to overcome before the summit.

At the top of the Hillary Step, I pulled myself up the last of the technical rock sections and found myself back on a hardened snow slope that angled up to the summit. As I looked up at the summit, my spirits lifted. At that point I knew we were going to make it to the top of the world.

25
The Summit

JANGBU WAS JUST BEHIND ME, AND THE TWO OF US WERE quite a distance ahead of Adam and Dad. I kept moving slowly up the slope, and even though I could see the summit, at our almost death-like pace it still took a considerable amount of steady trudging to reach it. It was a little bit frustrating to be so close but still only able to inch our way toward the top. Jangbu and I were filled with a new level of determination at that point, though, and we pushed on steadily until we finally stepped onto the summit!

On the summit of Everest was a monument made up of what appeared to be a large pile of intertwined flags. Most of them were Buddhist prayer flags, but there were also a few other flags and items climbers had left there.

I took my climbing pack off and clipped it to one of the ropes that was tangled in the mess of flags. I also clipped myself to one of the ropes just in case I slipped.

The summit was not very large, being about four feet wide by eight feet long, and it dropped off fairly steeply in all directions from that small plateau. One slip at the summit would likely be fatal in any direction.

Looking back, I could see that Adam and Dad had just passed the Hillary Step and were making their way to the summit as well. I took out our camera and took some photos of them as they approached. I also got Jangbu to snap a few photos of me, and I took a short video of him with the camcorder he was carrying.

We had finally achieved our goal. At around 8:00 a.m. on May 26, 2008, we reached the highest point on earth: the summit of Mount Everest.

It was pretty incredible to be there. Everywhere we looked, 360 degrees around us, everything was below us. The view from the summit was truly incredible, and the feeling of accomplishment that filled each of us was equally extraordinary. All the time and energy we had put into the expedition, finally culminating here, standing on the top of the world, was a dream come true.

We were not very organized while we were up there on the summit, and everything we did seemed to take a long time. We had put in every ounce of our hearts and souls for nearly two months to get to that point, and it was as if we were awestruck at actually having achieved such a momentous undertaking. We removed our oxygen masks temporarily and took turns taking a few photos of each other as well as a few group photos with our two Sherpas, Jangbu and Sangay.

Dad had brought a Rotary flag signed by all the members of his local Rotary club, so we took a few photos of that. I had brought a flag from the engineering company I worked for at the time and also one from a Toastmasters club that I was a member of. It was extremely difficult to get photos with the flags because the strong winds would bunch them up to the point that they were almost unidentifiable in most of the photos.

We had been there longer than we should have been, and Jangbu kept telling us that we needed to head down. We knew he was right, but we felt we had to get in everything we had planned to do on the summit, and it was a slow process.

We pulled out the satellite phone, and Dad made phone calls to Mom and to the president of his local Rotary club from the summit. When Dad was done with the satellite phone, he passed it to me.

I made a call to Natalie's cell phone and, although it was the middle of the night in Canada, she picked up because she had been waiting for the call just in case. We could hardly hear each other, and the phone call lasted less than thirty seconds, but it was good to hear her voice. My hands were nearly frozen because I had had to take my gloves off to dial the phone. By that time, Dad, Adam, and our two Sherpas had geared back up and were starting to head down. I wanted to make one more phone call: to the company I worked for, which had been quite supportive of the climb.

With nearly frozen fingers, I dialed the number I had written down. It went through to the complicated voicemail system, so I hung up and tried another number. I still couldn't get through to the person I had planned to leave the message for, so I tried a third time and just pushed zero until I got to the general mailbox. I left a message, and then I put the phone away and put my pack back on to head down after the others. My fingers were quite numb at that point from the cold, and I had lost feeling in the little finger of my right hand; I didn't get it back for a long time.

Although I had reminded myself countless times to turn off my oxygen regulator for the time we weren't wearing our masks on the summit, I forgot to do so, and so did Dad. We were all running on limited mental capacity, and it was very easy to make mistakes.

When I put my oxygen mask back on, I realized my blunder, and I remember thinking, "How stupid could I be?" given the fact that I had recited the reminder so many times. The oxygen mask was extremely uncomfortable and disgusting because the moisture from my breathing had pooled and frozen, and there were icicles all around the mask. The ring that contacted my face was completely iced up as well. I tried to bend it back and forth to break some of the ice away, and then with a shudder I jammed it back on my face and started to head down.

I was quite a distance behind the others when I left the summit. Sangay had waited for me and was only a little way ahead, but Adam and Dad were halfway to the Hillary Step.

26

A Close Call

IT FELT SO GOOD TO HAVE REACHED OUR GOAL, AND NOW WE were headed down. I was filled with an elated feeling of satisfaction and happiness — but the climb wasn't over yet.

I made fairly good time heading down the hard snow slope that led back to the Summit Ridge, and I had almost caught up to Sangay when I got to the Hillary Step and started lowering myself down.

Just as I finished climbing down the Hillary Step, I sensed that something was wrong. In a matter of seconds, my head got dizzy, and I collapsed on the ice beneath me. It didn't take me long to realize what was happening. I had run out of oxygen. I ripped off my mask and lay there on the ice, gasping for breath.

Because I had been exerting myself, it was totally different from when we had been resting on the summit. My body needed oxygen, and there was very little available. I gasped uncontrollably as I lay on the ice for what seemed like an eternity before I was finally able to control it to some degree. I had a long way to go to get to our spare oxygen cylinders on the South Summit, so I began to realize what a serious situation I could be in. I got up and tried to go down a bit farther, but before taking too many steps, I collapsed again onto my knees and started to feel a very weird cold sensation in my chest.

My limbs started wobbling and shaking uncontrollably. I knew it was not a good place to have that happen to me, as there was a 2,000-vertical-foot drop on both sides of the treacherous Summit Ridge. I tried a couple of times to move, but the shaking, dizziness, and the weird cold sensation kept getting worse, and I kept collapsing and gasping for breath.

Eventually, I turned to Sangay, who was not far away, and said, "I can't go on, I need oxygen." I am very thankful for Sangay at that point because, seeing the serious state I was in, he decided to give me his oxygen cylinder, which still had some oxygen remaining in it.

Because he was more experienced with climbing in the high altitudes than I was and had spent more time acclimatizing that year, he would potentially be a little better off without the oxygen than I would be, although it would still be very difficult for him.

I lay there on the ice, and Sangay went into my pack and switched our oxygen cylinders. When he had hooked up the regulator, I told him to turn it right up to three litres per minute. This was quite a high setting, as the maximum flow was four litres per minute. However, I wanted those terrible symptoms that I was experiencing to go away. He set the regulator and told me to keep going down.

I put my mask back on and attempted to head down, but the horrible sensations just continued to get worse.

That was when I really started to panic. I had probably spent longer than I should have on the summit, and I thought I was in serious trouble. I remember thinking to myself, "I'm on oxygen, and these symptoms are getting worse. I'm going to die up here on this ridge."

It wasn't such a crazy or unrealistic thought, as nearly 200 climbers had died before me in similar situations on Everest, and many of them would have experienced the exact symptoms I was feeling before those symptoms progressed to a fatal degree and claimed their lives.

My thoughts turned to 1996, the year fifteen people died on Everest, eight in one day. More particularly Rob Hall, one of the expedition guides, who had run out of oxygen on the Summit Ridge, did not have the energy to continue, and died, quite possibly right where I sat. It was all I could do to suppress these thoughts and images as my world started to crash.

I was continuing to panic, which just made things worse, because it takes energy to panic. I kept trying to tell myself to relax, but it wasn't working and my condition was continuing to deteriorate. I was stumbling and slipping and could hardly hold on to the shreds of rope as I clumsily struggled to go down a bit farther, with my extremities shaking uncontrollably.

I didn't make it very far at all before I came to where my father was. He had by now run out of oxygen as well and was leaning up against a wall of ice. I stumbled up to him and said, "Dad, I think I have HACE," which is the cerebral edema condition I mentioned earlier, where the blood vessels in the brain constrict and rupture. I was experiencing the onset of this serious high altitude condition, and it was quickly becoming a critical situation.

Dad had a steroid pill with him that we had brought for such emergencies. Steroids can help a little with climbers who are experiencing cerebral edema, although it is often a last resort. I thought that in the state I was in, it might be the only hope for me. I told Dad, though, that before we chose that option, he should go into my pack and turn my regulator right up to the maximum of four litres per minute.

I knelt down on the ice, and I remember just how frightened I was as he went into my pack. I knew that a rescue attempt from that altitude would be almost impossible. I would be dead long before they got me down to a safe altitude. I said a little prayer in my head that I would not die there, and I tried to control my racing panic.

To my great relief, when Dad went into my pack, he discovered that somehow the regulator had gotten screwed up and was malfunctioning, so there was no oxygen flowing at all. He never said exactly what the problem was and he doesn't remember anymore, but somehow the regulator had gotten set wrong or the line was pinched, and I wasn't receiving any flow to my mask.

With the oxygen masks we were using, it was difficult to tell from the feel of the mask if the oxygen was flowing or not. Because it was such a small amount of oxygen, I couldn't physically feel it on my lips or my face when it was on. However, my lungs could certainly tell the difference.

Thankfully, Dad was able to get the problem rectified and got the regulator set again to three litres per minute. Almost immediately, I started feeling better with the added oxygen, and my symptoms slowly started to subside.

It was a very frightening situation that I would never want to experience again. A lot of things go through your mind when you think you are about to lose your life.

At that point, though, we still had a serious situation on our hands because Dad had begun entering into the same state. He kept repeating that he also needed oxygen right away. I could appreciate how he must be feeling after my own terrible scare, and I headed off toward the South Summit, climbing down as fast as I could.

When I got to the South Summit, Jangbu was waiting, and I told him about Dad needing oxygen. He agreed to bring one of the spare bottles up, as he was most likely the quickest climber at that point. The whole process took a while though, and Dad slowly struggled his way down without oxygen for quite a distance before Jangbu got to him.

Eventually we all got back to the South Summit and were able to collect the few extra cylinders we had left there. The sun was bright by that time, and I had to switch from my goggles to my glacier glasses as we continued heading down.

The way down is considered by many climbers to be even more dangerous than the way up, for a few reasons. Our bodies were completely exhausted, and the brain-altering effects of oxygen depletion were debilitating. At that point, we had been climbing for over twenty-four hours without any sleep, and our bodies and minds were beginning to shut down.

It was still an extremely steep and technical descent, and we had to be very careful, especially on the exposed rock. I was thankful for the ropes because at one point on the ridge, I sleepily stumbled and fell forward down the side of the ridge. The rope broke my fall, and without it, I would have just kept falling, tumbling down the steep incline a few thousand feet to my death below.

After we had descended the steepest part of the ridge and it was beginning to level out a bit, we stopped to rest. We all lay down in the snow, and almost immediately my body went into a sleep state. Jangbu was quite cautious about resting and said it was not a good idea to rest there too long. In the exhausted state that we were in, it would have been too easy to fall asleep in an instant. He wisely convinced us that we should continue down before we had a chance to do much resting. We all knew it was the right thing to do, but it was so difficult to actually do it.

When we arrived at the Balcony, there were a few other climbers congregated there. The oxygen bottles that we had left at the Balcony were still partially full, and we had planned to collect them and bring them with us on our way down. However, there was a climber there who claimed that they were his own oxygen bottles, and we did not have the energy to argue with him, so we just left them for him. It was not a difficult decision to make because none of us really wanted to carry any extra weight down the steep South Face.

We did not stay very long at the Balcony before we bypassed

the others and started down.

It was tiring working our way down the South Face, and it was totally different being on the face during daytime. The steepness of the South Face was much more evident and somehow more real in the light of day.

It was also more dangerous going down because the climbers above would dislodge loose stones and rocks that would come sailing down the slope at near-terminal velocity. I tried to keep an eye out behind me to anticipate this, but it was hard to do all the time. Some of the rocks were quite large, and if they had hit me, I am sure they would have done some serious damage.

About halfway down the slope, we came across a deceased climber lying just to the side of the route. He was fully dressed in his mountaineering gear, fully frozen and preserved by the extreme cold. I would guess he had been lying there for several years, by the state of his jacket, but it was hard to say. I couldn't see his face because it was mostly covered in snow. But it was a sobering sight and a good reminder of the fact that we are human, and the fragility of life cannot be taken too lightly.

Of the more than 200 climbers that have lost their lives on Everest, the majority of the bodies are still in the Death Zone, where they remain, preserved by the immense cold, and will continue to remain, as if frozen in time, for hundreds of years. Many people don't understand how the bodies could be just left up there, year after year, without anyone retrieving them. The thing is that it would be almost impossible to bring a human body down from that altitude without an army of people to make it happen. The prospect of moving an object weighing a few pounds takes such an extreme effort that moving a full-sized human is out of the question.

Sometimes, if the bodies are near a crevasse, the Sherpas will push them into the crevasse to lay them to rest, but most of the time, they just remain where they died. The only exceptions are if family members want to make an attempt to retrieve the body of a dead climber or if the family can afford to hire a large group of Sherpas to try to bring the person down. It is a solemn situation, and though it doesn't seem right to leave them there, I think most climbers have such a love for climbing that they would probably want to be buried on the mountain anyway.

After a very long and extremely tiring descent, I finally arrived at the South Col, completely exhausted and barely able to keep my eyes open. I staggered over to our tent and collapsed inside. Laura was inside, and I was so exhausted that she had to help me get my boots off because I didn't have the energy to do anything. It had been over thirty hours since I had last slept, and I was completely spent.

The danger is that when you return to Camp 4, it is so easy to fall asleep instantaneously, due to pure and utter exhaustion, without properly checking and setting your oxygen regulator. Some climbers fall asleep without oxygen at Camp 4 and never wake up. It is very important that you are on oxygen and that your oxygen cylinder is not going to run out sometime during the night. My cylinder of oxygen was my lifeline at that point.

There are real hazards involved with sleeping in the Death Zone. Strange things can happen both physically and mentally. Frozen extremities are fairly common because of the extreme cold and reduced blood circulation throughout the body. We had to be very careful that our arms and hands were fully covered by our down jackets and large mitts and, whenever possible, were under the sleeping bag as well. Climbers have had to climb down with dead, frozen arms suspended above their heads or frozen in other positions, and many more have lost fingers and toes over the years.

The lack of oxygen often affects the mental state of the human mind as well and can cause odd sensations. This can make it seem like you are living in a dream world. Some climbers experience hallucinations and other bizarre effects.

27
Fearing the Worst

SHORTLY AFTER OUR RETURN TO CAMP 4, WE DISCOVERED
that an astonishing set of circumstances had changed everything for my sister, Laura. Laura had started out with us on
our summit attempt the previous evening but had returned to
Camp 4 when she was unable to continue. She had spent the
night there, connected to oxygen, and had rested the following
day on oxygen as well.

During that time, she had come to realize that she was
unlikely to have another chance to attempt the mountain, and
rather than resign herself to that, she began thinking that she
should find a way to give it another try. So after Dad returned
to Camp 4, Laura went to his tent to get his opinion.

At first, Dad thought that she must be crazy to want to
attempt the climb after seeing the exhausted and barely func-
tional states that we were in. However, he has usually trusted
our decisions, and he said that if she thought it was a good idea,
then she should go for it.

There were two major problems, however, that appeared
to be preventing her from making another summit attempt.
First, she had used up most of her allotted oxygen resting at
Camp 4 and did not have enough oxygen cylinders left to make
the attempt. Luckily, there was another climber in the Summit

Climb group who had turned around and given up before he had reached Camp 4. The group Sherpas had brought up a few bottles of oxygen for him and had left them at Camp 4. As he was not going to use them, Laura was able to make use of them instead, and her first problem was solved.

The second problem was that neither of our Sherpas could make another attempt at the summit. They were in much the same condition as Dad, Adam, and I, and they needed to get down to a lower altitude to recover. It seemed that this would prevent Laura from making another attempt. However, there was a lady from Singapore named Linda in the Summit Climb group who had paid a lot of money to have her own personal Sherpa during her climb.

Linda and her Sherpa, Pasang, had made their attempt at the summit the previous day, around the same time as us, but Linda had not been able to make it up the South Face. She had had to turn around partway up and head back to Camp 4. Therefore, Linda's Sherpa, Pasang, was still in reasonably good shape to continue climbing, as he had not expended very much energy the night before.

Laura and Linda had become quite good friends over the almost two months we had been climbing, and Linda decided to offer to have Pasang accompany Laura on the attempt. Linda also offered Laura her upgraded oxygen mask as well.

It was really quite fortuitous that both of these problems were resolved so easily. I wasn't able to stay awake to see Laura leave, but at eight-thirty that evening, she and Pasang headed off in the dark toward the South Face.

Adam and I were very groggy when we woke the next morning on May 27. It took us a long time to boil water and get ready, so we did not pack up and leave until later that morning.

Dad surprisingly got himself ready and left before us that morning. This was very out of the ordinary, and I think it must have been because he was in the tent with the Sherpas, and they wouldn't let him sleep in.

Dad and Jangbu had already left by the time Adam and I had packed up and left our tent. I was almost out of oxygen, but luckily Jangbu had managed to find a partial bottle and had left it for me to use.

Adam still had a partial bottle as well, so we were able to leave Camp 4, each having some oxygen to help us along.

By the time we left Camp 4, many of the tents had already been taken down. The climbing window is short on Everest, so everyone tries to make their attempt around the same time. If climbers are unsuccessful on the first try, they usually have to give up and go home. Very few climbers are able to make a second attempt in the same year. It is a sad thing for climbers to have to give up after having spent nearly two months working their way toward this one goal. However, that is the nature of the mountain and one of the things that makes it so difficult to conquer.

My legs still felt like jelly from the extreme effort I had put them through the day before. It was a slow and painful process making my way down the Geneva Spur and across the snowfield, but we weren't really in any hurry, so we just took our time.

Once we had descended the Yellow Band and were near the top of the Lhotse Face, I decided I would glissade down the Lhotse Face to try to save some of my energy. To glissade, you take your crampons off and sit on the snow with your knees bent so that you can slide down the slope on your backside, using your boots to steer and maintain control.

Usually glissading is done with the aid of an ice axe, and you drag the spike of the axe on one side or the other to control your direction and speed. The axe also acts as a safety device because if you lose control, you can roll over onto the axe, driving the pick of the axe into the snow, and stop yourself from falling. Climbers call this a self-arrest.

I had used this glissading technique frequently on Denali four years earlier to save my weary legs and to have a bit of fun on the way down. I never saw any other climbers using the technique on Everest or on Denali, though. I suppose it is because of the fear of losing control and sliding uncontrollably to one's death.

On the Lhotse Face, I did not have my ice axe, as I had not brought it up past Camp 2. It was far too steep to use an axe for glissading on the Lhotse Face anyway. However, I thought that it was safe enough to clip into the ropes and use them to control the speed of my descent. I wrapped the rope around my arm and behind my back so that when I rotated my arm, the friction would slow me down.

This worked quite well, and I found it to be fairly safe because, unlike on the way up, I was able to inspect all of the anchors and the condition of the rope before I put my trust in them. Adam did some glissading as well once he realized how effortless it was and how much easier it was than using his legs to lower himself down step by step.

When we reached Camp 3, we walked across the Lhotse Face to our tents. We had left some gear at Camp 3 that we needed to pick up. I had not had any water for a few hours at that point, so I lit one of the stoves and melted some ice. We spent about a half an hour at Camp 3, resting and melting water, before we gathered up our gear and moved on.

We should have heard from Laura that morning when she would be nearing the summit, but we did not. We tried to call her on the radio but got no response from her or Pasang. We were beginning to get very worried about her, especially because at that point there was nothing any of us would be able to do to help her if something was wrong. Even if we could have gone back up, which would not have been possible in the condition we were in, it would have taken us over twelve hours to get to her. We continued trying to contact her every hour or so, but as we descended and the minutes passed, we became more and more concerned.

It was quite difficult rappelling down the lower half of the Lhotse Face because the oxygen mask obscured my vision and fogged up my glacier glasses. However, it made the going that much quicker with the aid of the supplemental oxygen, so I did not want to take my mask off.

The sun was nice and warm above us, and we were able to take our time. I looked at my oxygen gauge, and since I still had a fair amount of oxygen, I turned the dial up higher than I really needed so as to make the descent even easier on me. I would not be needing the oxygen farther down, so there was no sense in letting it go to waste.

It still seemed to take forever before we finally rappelled down the final steep slope of the Lhotse Face and arrived on the upper part of the Khumbu Glacier.

Sections of the glacier had melted so much that they looked different than they had a few days earlier. There were sections where the snow had melted into hundreds of tiny icicles which stood up along the trail like stalagmites.

The path itself had melted quite far into the glacier in sections, usually because small rocks had fallen from the sides of the valley and had been heated by the sun. As we got closer to Camp 2, small glacial streams appeared everywhere around the trail.

Eventually, exhausted and sweaty, we arrived at the camp. Most of the other outfitters had already removed their tents and gear from Camp 2, and the camp looked a bit deserted.

At that point, it was after noon, and still nobody had heard anything from Laura. We were all extremely worried, especially Dad. We had been trying to call her on the radio all day, as had Arnold from Camp 2. Others had tried a number of times from Base Camp as well but with no reply.

As told by Dan Mallory:

I spent a relatively restful night at High Camp. I say *relatively,* as we had just gone thirty hours the day and night before during our summit push without sleep and with almost nothing to eat. However, this was a new day. This was the first day that we were not putting our complete heart and soul into our push to the top of Mount Everest. This was the day that we could reflect on our accomplishment and contemplate what it would mean in our future.

After gathering up all the gear in a relatively relaxed way, I set off from Camp 4 ahead of Adam and Alan, pondering how my daughter, Laura, was making out in her push to the top. I continued on through Camp 4 down the precipitous and daunting Geneva Spur with its almost vertical rock faces, but those concerns were secondary to the sense of satisfaction and elation that I was experiencing having just summited the highest mountain in the world. I continued on down the Yellow Band, traversing the 6,000-vertical-foot Lhotse Face to Camp 3, where I gathered up the remainder of my belongings that I had left a couple of days earlier.

As I was gathering up the gear, I was thinking about home, as I was sure that word would have gotten out that we were successful. It would be such an exciting time to be approached by all the different media, organizations, friends, and relatives wanting to know the whole story, and I could hardly wait to tell them. Adam and Alan were not too far behind, and I was thinking how great it was going to be for them. Very few people in the world had accomplished what they had just done, and I was so proud of their accomplishments and ready to tell the world of those accomplishments as well.

As I was descending by myself, alone, I had lots of time to think about what we had just done and in particular about Laura. She had been so sick with that gastrointestinal problem with incessant vomiting and diarrhea, and still she was willing and eager to make her own push for the summit. Her thinking to go for the summit was beyond belief to me after having thought back over how challenging and exhausting it was for us to reach the summit — how could it ever be possible for her to do it?

She had shown in the past how utterly incredible her stamina and endurance were — capable of a Herculean effort, no doubt. She is one incredible young lady, and I was very proud of her.

For our push to the top, we had set out at 8:30 p.m. in the dark. It had taken us eleven hours and forty-five minutes, which was an extremely good time. We had arrived at 8:15 a.m. on May 26. Laura had set out the previous evening at about 7:00 p.m., so I anticipated that in her debilitated state, she could reach the summit in fourteen hours.

Around 9:00 a.m., I took out our small family radio, the same radio that Laura and the boys would be carrying, and I called her. There was no answer, but it could just be that she was in a difficult spot to talk. So after about fifteen or twenty minutes, I placed the same call again; still no response.

There was a small twinge of anxiety, but I kept it well under control; she's so capable that I had complete confidence in her and her ultimate success. After another fifteen or twenty minutes, I tried again without success. I was starting to get a little concerned. We were on the same radio frequency as our outfitter at Base Camp and other outfitters.

Many climbers at Base Camp were familiar with the Mallory family who were climbing together, as it was unique, and we had a lot of people rooting for our safety and success. They heard me trying to reach Laura on a few occasions, and they were getting really worried. They knew that losing communication could mean that a very serious situation had developed. Any climbers who are left on that mountain for any extended period of time in the "Death Zone" would soon run out of oxygen, and death would shortly follow.

I was listening to the various calls that were sent out from Base Camp also trying to reach Laura. I knew that they would be doing a lot of praying and throwing of blessed rice, which they commonly do for safe passage. I was getting fearful. I continued to try to reach Laura on the family radio without delaying for long between calls, but with no success. I could not understand why we were not hearing from her. She had a radio, and so did her Sherpa — it did not make any sense.

I was going down the mountain on such a high from our accomplishment of reaching the summit, and at the same time I was almost cold with fear that something serious might have happened to Laura. My worst fear was that I would receive a call from Laura to say that she had fallen and had broken her leg or ankle and was needing me to come back up to help her. I was so tired, so totally exhausted, had not eaten to any extent for almost two days — but I would have gone back.

But I would not be likely to arrive in time. She would have run out of oxygen or sustained some other serious climbing accident before I got to her, and all that effort would have been wasted. I could not, absolutely could not contemplate or believe that I had lost my daughter on Mount Everest, but by now I could only think that was what had happened.

For seven hours while descending down the mountain toward Base Camp, I was trying to find the words to use to tell my wife that our daughter had died on Mount Everest. It was the worst day of my life! On the one hand, I had just reached the top of the world, and I was ready to tell the world. But on the other hand, the memory of that experience would only have brought back the painful memory of the death of our daughter. I could see that in the future I would not want any recollection of our Mount Everest expedition. I was being torn asunder by the extreme positions that I was dealing with.

———

28
Laura's Account

AS TOLD BY LAURA MALLORY:

I still remember moving forward like I was hardly moving at all. All I could see was Pasang, my Sherpa, and the two small circles of light from our headlamps in front of me. I was on my way toward the summit of Mount Everest, and I was determined not to give up.

To put my situation into perspective, I suppose I should back up a few days to when we had left Base Camp on what was to be our last push up the mountain.

The 3:00 a.m. wake-up call we had received at Base Camp on the morning of May 21 was very early, but I knew it was coming. I yelled at Dad to wake up and get moving, as it always took him longer to get ready. I had not been sleeping very much the previous few nights because I had developed a gastrointestinal problem that left me with very bad diarrhea. I had not been able to keep anything inside me for days, it seemed.

I remember thinking that I felt pretty good that morning, but I did not realize how weak I had become until we started climbing. It was our final push from Base Camp up the mountain, and I was not going to be left behind. We had spent two months on the mountain, training and getting acclimatized, and in spite of the nuisance, diarrhea was not going to stop me.

However, I will admit it did slow me down a bit.

Outside of Base Camp, I soon started to fall behind. Dad and Alan waited for me, but I kept having to stop to go to the washroom. At the top of the Khumbu Icefall, my diarrhea had become explosive with very little warning, and it was all I could do to get my climbing harness off in time. Dad and I stopped there at the top of the icefall for some lunch while Alan continued on up. We were there for about an hour so I could try to regain some of my strength and hydrate. It was a beautiful day, and I lay down and closed my eyes. I just felt spent. I was exhausted, and my body did not want to move.

I felt a bit better after a rest and drinking some liquids, so Dad and I continued on. The snow started falling just before reaching Camp 1. I felt like I was moving at a snail's pace, and soon I developed black diarrhea. As we continued upward, my brain clicked from nursing school, and I realized I was bleeding somewhere in my stomach or small bowel, as the black tar-coloured diarrhea was old blood. I realized at that point I needed advice from a doctor.

Dad radioed up ahead to Christian, and he confirmed that I was bleeding internally. Since Camp 2 was closer than turning back at that point, we asked if I could continue up rather then head back down through the icefall. He said I could, but I should be very careful. If a clot were to break loose, it could travel to my brain or even to my heart and cause serious damage or death.

My heart pounded as my nursing education kicked in and I realized the severity of my condition. I continued to get weaker as we climbed. I tried to keep pace with Dad, who was walking just ahead of me, but his pace was too fast, and I would have to stop every so often to rest.

Then the vomiting started. It came out as a black tar colour as well, and again it hit me how sick I was. All I wanted to do was to curl up and sleep and feel better. I wanted to be home in my bed with my mom taking care of me. But instead, I knew I had to keep climbing. I had no choice.

Dad again slowed his pace. Thankfully, the trail to Camp 2 was not as steep as other places on the mountain. After my vomiting episode, however, I was even weaker, and it was taking me even more time to continue because I was stopping more frequently.

Adam had heard how sick I was and decided to come down with some water and medication for me. When he arrived, I was so thankful. I could hardly move. He took my pack from me and even had me hold his harness so he could help pull me up. We worked our way slowly upwards together one step at a time. With the encouragement of both Dad and Adam, I was able to make it to Camp 2.

I was so exhausted when we arrived. Dad helped me get into the tent and get ready for bed. A climb that should have taken me eight hours had taken almost twelve.

I was given hot water to rehydrate, a strong antibiotic, erythromycin, and antacid pills. Almost immediately after I took the medicine, I was fast asleep.

We spent several days at Camp 2, and I did recover my strength after those rest days, but that was not the end of my problems.

The climb from Camp 2 to Camp 3 was difficult and left me quite tired, but the climb from Camp 3 to Camp 4 nearly killed me. Being sick had slowed me down and took a lot out of me.

When I finally arrived at Camp 4, I did not know where to go. It was several hours after Dad, Adam, and Alan had arrived. Finally I got directions from Dad, who told me which tent Alan and Adam were in, and I slowly half-crawled, half-walked over to them. It was very windy, and I had to struggle against the wind to make it to the tent.

Arriving, I collapsed in the tent with Adam and Alan. They gave me something to drink and eat. I really wanted to rest,

The shadow of Mount Everest on the surrounding mountains.

Adam climbing on the Southeast Ridge.

On the South Summit looking up at the Summit Ridge to the peak of Everest.

Climbing on the Summit Ridge with Dad and Adam.

Standing on the summit of Mount Everest with Dad and Adam.

Sitting down to make my phone calls.

Adam and Dad starting the descent.

Beginning my descent of the Summit Ridge.

Holding my lifeline as I finally let myself fall asleep.

Glissading down the Lhotse Face.

Lowering myself down a steep section of the Lhotse Face.

Laura with Pasang before heading out on her summit attempt.

Laura nearing the summit.

Laura at the summit of Mount Everest.

Dad giving Laura a big hug at Base Camp.

Safely back at Base Camp.

Very happy to be back at Base Camp.

A flowering tree on the way out from Base Camp.

A remote canoeing and hiking trip to celebrate Dad's birthday in 2016.

Hiking the Torres del Paine circuit in Southern Chile with Natalie.

A red rock adventure with Natalie in the American Southwest.

Mountain biking in early spring with Aria and Oaklan.

The 1921 Everest Expedition Base Camp: George Mallory back row right.
(A.F.R. [Sandy] Wollaston / Wikimedia Commons)

but there wasn't much time for that. We were supposed to be leaving in a few hours for the summit. I was exhausted. I was wondering if I was going to be able to make it. The boys helped me a little, trying to get some water and food into me, but there was not much food available at the camp, and they were exhausted and did not have that much energy.

The wind whipped around the tent, making the inside very noisy. I felt like I was yelling at Adam and Alan most of the time so they could hear me. After some warm water and some soup, I managed to curl up next to them and close my eyes, although it was difficult to sleep with the noise and the oxygen mask on.

It was not a long rest before we started to get our bags packed and to put our gear on to head out in the dark on our summit attempt. I kept hoping that it would be too windy or something would come up and we would have to wait until the following day, but nothing came. I packed a few extra clothes just in case I needed them, but mostly it was an empty pack so I could carry my oxygen cylinders.

I pulled on my long underwear and fleece pants and then my green down-filled suit. I stuffed a water bottle inside my jacket next to my body to keep it from freezing. It was incredible how warm the down suit was, and with the strong, steady wind and the cold temperatures, it was definitely needed. At around eight-thirty that night, in the dark with only our headlamps to guide us, we started out, picking up our oxygen cylinders and walking slowing away from the camp.

My heart started pounding as we began walking. I had not had much time that day to see what the terrain looked like, so I was heading out in the dark on unseen terrain. My stomach churned from the nerves, and butterflies flew around in my body. I had not had any diarrhea for a couple of hours at that point, and I was hoping it was out of my system. Still, I was not feeling well, and I was anxious about what was to come.

As I trudged away from the tents, my legs wobbled

underneath me from the weak state they were in, and my crampons twisted, scratched, and slipped on the rocky landscape beneath me.

Soon we were past all the tents and continuing out into the darkness. I could see the three headlamps of my brothers and father in front of me as well as those of our two Sherpas. It seemed like I was going backwards, because I was moving so slowly and they seemed to be getting farther and farther away from me so quickly. I tried to walk a little quicker, but my legs would not move. I felt sick and weak, and for an instant I lost focus on where I was stepping. My feet slipped from under me and down I fell, crashing onto the rocks under me. My bowels let loose a little as well, and I knew at that moment that I was not going to be able to continue.

One of our Sherpas, Sangay, saw me fall and came back to help me. I was so weak at that point that I could hardly move. I lay on the ground for several moments, trying to regain my strength. Sangay encouraged me to get up and keep going, but it was no use. I knew I was not going to be able to go on with the others. My heart sank as I pulled out my radio. I told Dad that I had just fallen and that I was still sick with more diarrhea and I did not have the strength to continue on. He said he understood. With a heavy heart, I turned around while the others continued on up.

Terror stuck me at that point. As the others continued up, I was left alone in the dark. Camp 4 was somewhere in front of me, but I was too far away to see it with my headlamp. I started walking in what I thought was the right direction, and my heart beat faster with every step as I walked forward without seeing any tents. What if I were going in the wrong direction? They would find my body the next day somewhere on the South Col, cold and exhausted or maybe even dead. Or perhaps they might never find my body at all.

Finally, with a sigh of relief, I saw the first tent. I walked toward it as the wind whipped against my back. When I arrived at the first tent, I realized it was not ours. I began hunting for our tent, and it took me several tries before I found it.

I crawled in, completely exhausted, and stripped off my soiled clothes. I cleaned up, put fresh underwear on, and crawled into my sleeping bag to get warm. As I lay there in the tent by myself, the decision I had just made hit me, and I began to cry. Tears streamed down my cheeks as I realized that I would not be summiting Mount Everest with my family and that I likely would not achieve my goal at all.

I thought about all my family and friends at home who were counting on me to reach the summit, and now I had let them down. I looked back at the two months I had just spent on the mountain and how much strength, both physical and mental, it had taken for me to get to Camp 4, only to have to give up and turn back. I was disappointed in myself, but I also knew I had made the right decision. I knew physically and mentally that I was not well enough or strong enough to have continued on. If I had forced myself to continue, something terrible would have happened. I soon fell asleep, crying in the darkness, with my oxygen mask on and my oxygen cylinder beside me.

In the morning, I woke early to the wind beating against my tent. The sun was up, and I could hear people talking in the tent next to mine. I listened closely and soon recognized the voice of Linda, a fellow climber who was part of the Summit Climb group. I called over, and soon we were having a conversation between the two tents. She invited me over to her tent, but first I wanted to hear how the boys were doing. I got on the portable radio and called to them. It was not long before Dad got on the radio saying they were fine and near the summit and would call again when they reached the top. I crawled out of my tent after getting dressed in my high altitude clothing, and with my oxygen tank in hand, I made my way over to Linda's tent.

I spent most of that day with Linda and her Sherpa, Pasang.

We boiled water and drank tea and soup to keep hydrated. It was nice having company and someone to talk to about what had happened the night before. She explained to me her situation and that she had tried to make an attempt at the summit the previous night as well but her Sherpa thought she was moving too slowly and would not make it to the summit in time, so they had turned around. We tried to comfort each other from the disappointments we both had had the night before.

It was not long before I again heard Dad's voice on the radio to explain that he, Alan, and Adam, along with the two Sherpas, had summited. I was so excited and thrilled for them, but it was hard to celebrate, knowing that I was not able to be up there with them. I was feeling a great deal better that morning, and I was hoping that if everything worked out, I would be able to try for another summit attempt that night. However, I had two problems that soon became clear to me.

Around lunchtime, I got on the radio to talk to Arnold to see about the possibility of making another summit attempt that night. He soon gave me the bad news that there were no more Sherpas to climb with me and that there might not be enough oxygen available either.

My heart sank even further at his response. I was feeling much better and wanted to go, but now again I would be unable to.

Linda saw my disappointment and suggested that her Sherpa, Pasang, climb up with me. I was not sure of the idea at first because she had paid a lot of extra money to have Pasang with her for the whole climb. Pasang was in agreement because he wanted to climb, but I was not sure I felt right about leaving Linda alone.

As much as I argued with her, she insisted, and soon Pasang and I were discussing plans. I then had to deal with the second of the problems that faced me — the lack of oxygen cylinders. I had used one of my bottles up spending an extra day at high camp, so I was short one bottle for the summit attempt. I knew there were people that had not made it up to High Camp in the Summit Climb group, and I was hoping that I would be able to use one of their cylinders. Once I had talked to Arnold again and confirmed that indeed there were extras, I figured I was ready. Unfortunately, the politics started.

The Sherpa who had originally brought up the extra bottle I was going to be using accused Pasang of reaping the benefits of the hard work he had done. Pasang did not want to cause trouble, so he backed out of accompanying me because of what the other Sherpa had said.

I again talked to Arnold to try to sort the situation out. I thought it was silly that I had what I needed but, because of politics between Sherpas, was not able to accomplish or try to accomplish what I had come there for. Arnold came on the radio and talked to both of the Sherpas in Nepalese, and finally, after several long minutes of conversation that I did not understand, Pasang again agreed to climb with me.

I returned to my tent late that afternoon to try to get my things organized for the ascent later that night. I went out to collect more snow to melt for drinking water, and I decided not to take oxygen, thinking it would be easier. That was a mistake. I was exhausted when I returned to the tent and collapsed, out of breath. It took me several minutes to recover and regain my composure. I was soon melting snow and getting ready for the climb.

At around four that afternoon, I saw the boys coming down the mountain. It was a slow process, but finally they arrived in camp. Dad came in first and was exhausted, so he hardly said anything to me before collapsing into his tent. Alan came next, completely spent as well. He collapsed into our tent, and I had to help him take his boots off and get into his sleeping bag. Adam was last, and all he wanted was water. I gave him some of the water I had just boiled and then helped him into the tent, too.

I was worried about them. They could hardly talk and were almost delirious with exhaustion. I had never seen anyone so worn out before and so out of breath. It made me worry if they were going to be okay, but I knew I had to stay focused and get myself ready for the climb.

When I told Adam and Alan what I was planning to do, they looked at me a little strangely but did not say much. Just before seven that night, when Pasang and I were getting the last things ready, I went over to Dad's tent to say goodbye and see what he thought of my heading up. At first Dad looked at me like I was nuts, but then he told me that if I felt good, he knew I could do it if I was healthy. Those words of his empowered me. He had told me what I needed to know to make my own decision.

At around seven that night, with oxygen and headlamps, Pasang and I left the camp. I was feeling a lot better, and my strength had partially returned. It was light out to begin with, so we didn't need our headlamps at first. There were no fixed ropes as we started the ascent, but it was a beautiful night with not much wind.

It was fairly cold, but as we got moving, my down-filled suit and my thick gloves kept me warm. The gloves were actually too warm at times, and I had to take them off periodically because my hands were sweating.

The hard snow crunched under my feet as the crampons dug deep. I moved ahead, leading the way for the first part of the climb with Pasang following close behind me. When we arrived at the starting point of the fixed ropes, we had been climbing for quite a while. The ropes led up a steeper section for which we had to clip in and use our Jumar ascenders.

At that point, I encouraged Pasang to lead the way so I would have someone to follow and keep pace with. I found that if I could walk at the same pace as someone else, I was able to move quicker and stop less frequently.

Pasang led the way, and soon we were in full darkness. The

terrain was difficult to make out, as it was a very dark night, and I could see only a few feet in the direction that my light was shining. I do remember coming to a crevasse that we had to climb around, even though the ropes went across it. Thankfully, there was enough slack in the rope to go around the outside and carry on upwards without having to climb in and out of the crevasse.

As the darkness loomed around us and the snow started to fall, I became very nervous and scared. I could see lightning in the distance, and this added to my nervousness. My heart started pounding in my chest. Would I be caught in another lightning storm like I had been caught in on Mount Elbrus?

The memory flashed into my head. Climbing in Russia, with my dad a few yards in front of me and white clouds all around us, I could hear the sound of the electricity going through the air. "Dad," I yelled, "are you sure we're not going to be struck by lightning?" As I waited for a reply, I could feel the hair on the back of my neck rise. "Dad, the hair on my neck feels like it's standing on end."

Dad's reply sounded quite urgent: "Laura, dig your poles into the snow as deep as you can, as they have metal on them, and get down as low as you can to the ground!"

As quickly as I could, I crouched to the ground and dug my poles in as deep into the hard-packed snow as I could. I closed my eyes and began praying, "Please, Lord, help us survive this storm and make it off this mountain." The wind and snow whipped around us, but closer to the ground, we could no longer hear the electricity in the air, and my body stopped tingling and my hair stopped standing on end. We waited for quite a while, crouched together, shivering on the ground, before the storm finally passed.

But this was a different mountain.

On several occasions, I remember asking Pasang if it was safe to continue. He would nod and keep climbing. At that point, I had to trust him and put my life in his hands. He knew more about the mountain than I did, and I really wanted to continue, even though I was terrified.

I was very relieved when we moved above the snowy weather and into the clear darkness. On several occasions, I thought I could see headlamps below us, but they disappeared, and I wondered if some people had turned around because of the weather.

After many hours, which seemed like an eternity, Pasang and I reached the Balcony. I could see where many people had left cylinders of oxygen there for the way back down, but Pasang and I decided against that and carried all of our oxygen cylinders with us. However, Pasang and I did stop at the Balcony to have a rest and drink some liquids. The only thing easily accessible and still warm was tea that Pasang had brought, so we drank that.

It did not take long, sitting at the Balcony, for my body to start to cool down, and we soon had to continue in order to keep warm. Not long after we left the Balcony, my first bottle of oxygen ran out. Pasang hooked up my second bottle and increased the oxygen flow to 2.5 litres per minute.

We soon reached a very steep section that we had to climb. Looking at it, I realized that before I attempted it, it was time for me to have a pee.

It is hard enough for a woman to squat without a toilet, but to make matters worse, I was wrapped up in a climbing harness and high-altitude climbing clothing. I had waited until the last possible minute before I had to pee because I knew how cold it would be and the amount of work it would be to get the harness down far enough not to get myself drenched. Unfortunately, I waited too long; when my body felt that cool temperature, it was hard to hold it in anymore, and I wet my pants a little. I was worried that this would make me colder, but actually it did not bother me at all.

As I was stopped on the ridge peeing, Pasang had continued up the steep section, and now I had to tackle it on my own. It was almost vertical with rocks and snow sections mixed together intermittently. There were many old ropes from years past, and I was not sure which path was the best to take. I ended up grabbing several ropes, hoping one would hold, and started climbing. I was actually thinking I was on the Hillary Step, but I was far from it. I slowly worked my way through the rocks and snow. I was getting tired at that point and was worried that I might slip. Pasang was not there to show me where to place my feet, and I kept looking above, hoping to see a clear path.

A group of climbers, whose headlamp lights I had seen below me earlier, soon caught up and were then stuck behind me. They were an American group, and I remembered having met them before lower down. Their guide was very nice and gave me some encouragement and some ideas as to where to place my feet. With his help, I was able to continue moving up the mountain slowly and got to an area on the steep ascent where the American group was able to pass me. I took guidance from their lead, moving slowly up the wall behind them, and at the top, Pasang was waiting for me.

The sun was rising at that point, and I started to see silhouettes of the mountains around me. I could see it was going to be a beautiful day. The wind was still not very strong, and Pasang and I moved slowly and steadily. At that point, I could see the South Summit. The snow was loose right before the South Summit, and I kept sliding backwards. However, once through that section, Pasang and I climbed up a small incline and arrived at the South Summit.

The South Summit was amazing. From there, I could see the snow-covered peaks of the mountains all around me and the summit of Everest that lay before me. I looked at the ridge that was my next challenge and cringed. The ridge had some very steep sections; on one side, it had a near-vertical drop-off, and the other was not much better. I could see the American team partway along the ridge, all moving very slowly. I knew that I would have to challenge the ridge, but my spirits were high because I was getting closer to the summit. It did not look that far from where we were to the summit, but I had been warned that it was at least another two hours of climbing.

Pasang and I each left a bottle of oxygen at the South Summit and decided to rehydrate before attempting the ridge. Since I had a warm bottle hidden in my jacket, we decided to drink from it. The problem was that my jacket was stuck, frozen from the moisture and saliva dripping from the oxygen mask. However, with effort from both of us, we were able to push the bottle up and squeeze it through the small opening at the top of my jacket. It must have looked hilarious if anyone had been there to see. I was pushing, and Pasang was pulling from the top, and I was trying not to get strangled at the same time.

Finally, after some effort, we were able to get the bottle out. We both took long drinks before I had to again squeeze the bottle back down my jacket and try to get it into the inside pocket. It was too difficult to get it into the pocket, so I left it held tight to my body where it could not move.

The Summit Ridge was the hardest part of the climb. At that point, I had been climbing for twelve hours and was getting very tired. The lack of oxygen coupled with the treacherous terrain made the ridge a nightmare to climb. There were fixed ropes along the ridge, but the ridge was a mix of rock and snow, and a lot of the ropes were old and tattered. My crampons slid across the rocks, and I had to take my time and focus. That was where I needed to concentrate the most, because a little mistake could easily result in very serious consequences.

The wind was stronger on the ridge, and it was hard to hear

Pasang as he gave me directions where to place my feet or move my hands. We constantly had to yell at one another to be heard.

Just before the summit was a gradual incline. I saw Pasang pull out our portable radio and start talking into it. I figured he had called Base Camp and informed them we were okay and had just reached the summit. I didn't think much more about it, as I was more concerned about just trying to put one foot in front of the other.

On May 27, 2008, I became the youngest Canadian female to summit Mount Everest, and, as well, the four of us became the first family of four in the world to summit.

The rope ended as I reached the summit, and I had to concentrate on my walking as I walked around the summit, taking in the views on all sides of me. It was breathtaking, and everything was below me. It was a beautiful day with hardly a cloud in the sky. I had made it! I had made it to the top of the world. I did not know what to do or how to feel. I was so extremely exhausted, and I was just so glad to be there, but I was just praying that I would have the strength to get back down.

Pasang and I stayed at the summit for about twenty-five minutes. I wanted lots of pictures and a few videos, and I also wanted to take in the scenery. I had enough time to leave my signature pair of underwear at the summit before Pasang told me we needed to be going. I have left a pair of underwear at the top of Mount Elbrus and Mount Kilimanjaro, so it was tradition to do so on Everest.

The way down seemed harder than the way up. I was so exhausted that it was all I could do to concentrate on the steps I was taking. The Hillary Step came soon after leaving the summit, and it took me several tries to figure out my footing and to feel comfortable before I was able to make it down the vertical face of rock and ice. Pasang kept giving me ideas, but I realized after I had tried a couple of his ideas that I needed to figure out what was comfortable for me.

We continued down, and I had started to lose focus when I slipped on a flat rock and fell, almost sliding off the rock and thousands of feet down the side of the ridge. I tried to regain my focus after that, and I knew I had to concentrate or I was not going to make it off the mountain. It was all I could do to secure each foothold and grab the rope with my hands.

Finally we reached the South Summit and were off the summit ridge. I was glad to arrive there because I had just run out of oxygen. Pasang located our cylinders and started to switch them. He played around with them for several minutes before he realized that the threads were stripped on one of the bottles. This meant that the bottle was useless and we were unable to use it. I started to panic because my body was slowly starting to get cold from the inside out, and I could hardly move any of my limbs without great effort.

It is amazing how quickly your body starts to slow down without the necessary oxygen it requires. Pasang started picking up cylinders around us, hoping that one of them might have something in it. He ended up going down into a small crevasse where many old oxygen cylinders had been stored, hoping to find one that was full. Thankfully, we were in luck; he found a partly full cylinder. God had blessed us, and we hooked it up and continued our descent.

The climb down was like a blur. I was so exhausted and was using all the strength I had left in me to focus on each step I was taking so as not to fall or catch my crampons on something. Just above the Balcony, Pasang and I stopped to rehydrate. The day was beautiful and actually relatively warm. The wind was still minimal, and the sun's rays beamed down on us.

I asked Pasang if he had notified Base Camp that we had summited, and he shook his head no. I asked him who he had spoken with on the radio, and then he pulled out the radio and explained in his broken English that the batteries were dead. This meant that for nearly twenty-four hours, no one had heard from us. I took a look at the radio to see if anything could be done to make it work, but indeed it was dead. I knew I was okay, but I was worried about what Dad and the boys were going through, not hearing from us. I had left my radio at Camp 4, so there was nothing we could do at that point.

We continued down, and around 4:00 p.m. that afternoon, we stumbled back into Camp 4. In the tent, Pasang and I both collapsed. He found a radio and called down and told everyone we were okay and had been to the summit and arrived back safe and sound.

We both drank a bit before falling fast asleep, exhausted. I woke several hours later, shivering. I had not gotten into my sleeping bag and was very cold because I was just wearing my down-filled suit. Pasang also woke and headed to the next tent, where he prepared some tea and soup. It was late in the evening, and since there was no one in the other tent, Pasang decided to sleep in it so it would not blow away.

Alone in the dark in my tent, I was filled with mixed emotions. I was so happy that I had summited, but I had no one to share it with. I decided to figure out how to use our satellite phone and give my mother a call.

There was no answer at our home, so I called her cell phone. She said when she picked up the phone and realized it was me, she nearly drove off the road. She did not know that I had been trying to summit that day and was thrilled to hear that I had made it and was back safe at Camp 4.

It was so great to hear my mother's voice and tell her a bit about my climb. When I got off the phone, I was on a high. My mother was so proud of me for what I had done, and I was able to tell her about it. Again, though, I was back in the dark, in the cold, in a tent by myself. I got organized and crawled into my sleeping bag and fell fast asleep.

I awoke only once in the night with the tent a foot away from my face. The wind had picked up during the night on the South

Col and was so strong it was caving the tent in on me. My heart leapt into my throat before I was able to regain my composure. There was nothing I could do, and I was not going to blow away. I stuck with that hope, and back off to sleep I fell.

———

29

Down through the
Last of the Hazards

THERE WERE NOT A LOT OF CLIMBERS STILL AT CAMP 2. ONLY the outfitter leader, Arnold, and the cook remained, as everyone else had been sent back to Base Camp due to acute cases of diarrhea. We each had our own tent that evening because of the few people that were there. I tried to eat something before going to sleep, but I wasn't really able to stomach much.

I wanted to make sure that I got up early the next morning for the last descent through the Khumbu Icefall. With the warmer weather, the icefall was doing a lot of moving and was very dangerous. It was very important to leave well before the sun rose the next morning. I didn't have an alarm clock in my tent, so I spoke to Adam and Dad, and they said they would set their alarms and wake me up as soon as they got up so that we could get an early start. After lying for a few minutes in my tent, I fell fast asleep.

By the time I woke up, it was already very late in the morning, and it was quite bright out. I went out of the tent immediately when I woke and was just in time to see Adam and Dad walking away from the camp. They had already woken up, eaten breakfast, and packed all their gear and were heading down.

I shouted at them to ask why they hadn't woken me up like they had said they would, but they just smiled and said they had thought that I had already left. They thought it was humorous because they knew how seriously I had taken the icefall crossing in the past. I was quite angry because it put my life in additional danger, but I suppose it was partly my fault for not having a method of my own for waking myself.

I packed up my equipment as fast as I could and geared up to leave. I had a huge amount of weight in my pack because I had to pack everything I had brought in the two times we had climbed up to Camp 2, to bring down in one shot.

I left as soon as I could. It wasn't very easy to move because I had a lot of weight on my back and some loose items tied onto the outside of my pack as well that kept flopping back and forth.

I climbed down as fast as I could, and I was able to catch up to and pass Adam and Dad before they arrived at Camp 1. I quickly continued on past them, but the sun was already quite high in the sky when I reached the Khumbu Icefall. I was really wobbly going across the ladders because of the weight on my back, but my lungs were well conditioned from being exposed to the low oxygen levels at the top of Everest, so I was able to move very quickly in the more oxygen-rich air.

When I made it out of the most dangerous part of the icefall, I knelt down and said a small prayer of thanks that nothing bad had happened to me in the six times I had passed through that risky expanse. At that point, I was away from the real danger, and I started to relax and slow down a bit.

With the heavy pack on my back, I had exhausted my legs by going down through the icefall so fast. My legs and the rest of my body felt very unsteady as I trudged my way across Base Camp to where our tents were. I was able to weigh my pack when I arrived at the mess tent, because one of the Sherpas had found a weigh scale. My pack weighed forty pounds (eighteen kilograms) at that point.

After dropping my pack, I went back to the mess tent to replenish my fluids and wait for Adam and Dad. A little over two hours later, they arrived.

Dan Mazur was at Base Camp and had had some beers brought up to the camp as well as some Finlandia vodka. After eating some dinner, we sat in the mess tent with the other climbers who were still at Base Camp and drank a beer. We then commenced passing around the vodka for everyone to have a few swigs straight from the bottle.

Dan Mazur and many of the climbers were very jolly by the time the Finlandia bottle was empty, and we all had a good time and some good laughs.

We stayed up quite late socializing in the mess tent, and I had no problem falling asleep after I finally bid everyone goodnight and headed off to my tent. It was great to finally relax and to feel such a sense of accomplishment and relief, which put a smile on my face. I slept like a baby that night.

The next morning, I woke up with my muscles feeling quite stiff. Temba brought me tea, but I fell asleep again midway through drinking it, and he had to come back and wake me up again for breakfast.

At 11:00 a.m., completely exhausted but very happy, Laura arrived. It was a relief that she had made it back unharmed, and Dad gave her a big hug, as he had promised to do when he had heard that she was okay on the radio the previous day.

It was a great feeling when we all were safely back at Base Camp. We had come back down through a lot of risky sections of the mountain, but now we were out of the real danger zone and we could finally relax. All we wanted to do was to get as far from the mountain as we could.

We uploaded some pictures to the Internet using Dan Mazur's laptop and satellite connection, and then I started organizing and packing the gear in my tent.

It was a fairly uneventful and lazy day overall, filled mostly with resting and waiting.

30

The Way Out

ON MAY 30, I WOKE UP AND PACKED THE REST OF MY belongings to depart Base Camp and start heading down. I was very glad to be leaving. After almost two months of calling Base Camp my home, I had had about enough of it and was overjoyed to finally be heading toward civilization.

I was hoping to leave right after breakfast, but it took a long time because everyone wanted to take group photos, and Dad wanted other photos of us at Base Camp as well. It was probably a good idea that we stayed there and took the photos because we got some good ones of us looking like weathered and worn mountain climbers. My face was badly burnt and peeling, and Adam, Dad, and I all had big, bushy beards.

Finally, just before noon, I said my last goodbyes, and Laura and I set off. As we walked through the camp for the last time, it looked totally different. Everything was melting or had already melted, and there were small streams bubbling through the rock and ice. Many of the tents had already been removed, and there were only a few climbers still remaining.

We moved very fast that day as we hiked down. We had just spent two months building red blood cells, and our bodies had a lot of excess capacity at that point, so we were able to trek at a very fast pace, nearly running, and our hearts were barely even beating. In effect, during the two months we had been on the mountain acclimatizing, we had done what could be considered as natural blood doping. We got the same effect that some Olympic athletes get by blood doping, but we did it naturally. As we headed down, we were descending into an oxygen-rich environment, and we felt nearly superhuman.

I remember my legs having a real problem, though. Because of the very long climbing days we had been having and the small amount of food we were able to eat, our bodies had used up all of our fat supplies and had started burning muscle to create energy. Each of us had lost about thirty pounds (thirteen kilograms) during the climb, and for that reason I was very thin, and my muscles were getting sore from the rapid descent.

The scenery on the way down was beautiful. It was almost summer by that point, and the Khumbu Valley had come alive. There were many different flowering trees along the way as well as a lot of colourful birds. Dad especially enjoyed the different species of birds, as he had studied them as a hobby for most of his life.

We went all the way down to Pangboche, a distance of about fifteen miles (twenty-four kilometres), that first day of our trek out from Base Camp. My leg muscles hurt during the last part of that descent, and when we finally arrived at the Sonam Lodge in Pangboche, I was certainly glad we didn't have to go any farther. Dad and Adam arrived in Pangboche a few hours later and were equally glad to stop for the night.

We met a university professor from Ohio at Pangboche who was quite taken by our story of being the first family of four to make it to the top, so he bought a box of wine to celebrate with us. That night was a lot of fun, and we laughed and danced late into the night.

We left the Sonam Lodge quite late the next morning for our long day of trekking to Namche, where we stayed in the Thamserku Lodge. We were very tired so we went to bed early.

After breakfast, we left the lodge and went to the Namche Internet café in order to send our friends and family a few emails. We also emailed some questions to Deha about departure logistics, and then we started off again.

The trek from Namche to Lukla that we did that day was extremely long and energy draining, because we trekked about eleven miles (eighteen kilometres). What made it worse is that after we passed Pakding, it was an uphill climb back up to Lukla. That long day almost killed my legs. They were incredibly sore, and my leg muscles started going into spasms and locking up during the last part of the trek. When I finally arrived at the Namaste Lodge in Lukla, I had to keep my legs straight for the remainder of the evening, or else I would experience muscle locking. It was very painful, and I had a very awkward, uncomfortable evening, but I was glad to be there and couldn't wait to leave and get away from the Himalayas.

In the morning, we registered too late to take the first Yeti Airlines flight back to Kathmandu, but we managed to get on the second. It is a good thing we did; they didn't allow any more flights out of Lukla for a few days after that because the weather turned bad.

During the flight, we got to experience some of the incoming bad weather. The plane bumped and jolted every direction due to the high winds, and it was a relief when it finally touched down at the Kathmandu airport.

It seemed like all the four of us did was eat for those first few days back in Kathmandu. The hotel we checked into had a breakfast buffet, and we took full advantage of it.

Our return flights to Canada were still a few weeks away because when we had originally booked them, we didn't know the exact date when we would be getting off the mountain, and we wanted to make sure we had adequate time.

As none of us really wanted to spend any more time in Kathmandu, one of the first things we did was go to the airline and get our flights changed. The earliest flight we could change to was still a week away, but we took it.

For the remaining week, we spent a few days exploring Kathmandu and then a few days in the Chitwan jungle. The jungle was quite interesting, as we rode elephants and saw some incredible wildlife. Normally it would have been a great place to vacation, but at that point, all we wanted to do was get home.

Finally, the day of our departure arrived. It was so nice to be finally heading home that my spirits were high that day, and the departure time couldn't come fast enough. As we boarded the aircraft, it felt like we were saying our last goodbyes to a culture and a way of life that had become our reality for the lengthy time that we were there. It had been an incredible experience and is one that I do not regret, although it was definitely time to be home.

31

A Brief Reflection

A FEW YEARS LATER, AS I LOOK BACK ON THE CLIMB, IT almost seems surreal what we undertook and were able to accomplish as a family. We successfully reached the highest point on earth and, most important, we all returned safely. It was a monumental accomplishment for each of us and one we will remember for the rest of our lives.

When we were physically climbing the mountain, we were so engrossed in the activity and focused on what we were doing, pushing ourselves toward our goal step by step, that we didn't really have time to reflect on what was actually happening and what it all meant.

For me, the draw of Everest had always been about actually reaching my objective of physically standing on the summit. Many people talk about how it is the journey that counts more than the end goal, but I have to admit that for me it was initially never about the experience.

I had flown to Nepal for one reason, and that was to reach the mark I had set for myself and then return home. Pushing my body and mind to new levels was all part of it, and I learned a lot along the way, but it was all simply a series of necessary stepping-stones toward the personal gratification and fulfillment that only the summit could bring.

Now, some years later, I have come to realize more and more that the journey truly is the part to be experienced and savoured in any endeavour and, in many cases, is in fact more important than the result. However, at the time I had a very rigid focus, and that is all I allowed myself.

It is an odd but special human sensation that is generated when you reach a major goal you have set for yourself. A profound feeling of satisfaction and sense of completeness surfaces from deep within. It is almost like when the mind has set its sights on a target, there is an emptiness of sorts created that cannot truly be filled until the target has been reached.

I find this to be especially true in my own mind and body. It is almost as though I need or take pleasure in continuously having ambitions in my life to strive toward. I suppose it is almost an addiction, of sorts, to the feeling of satisfaction that is generated. However, I don't look at it as a negative addiction at all, because it gives me energy and adds purpose and vigour to my daily thoughts and actions.

I don't know if it is a universal trait to strive to set and achieve goals, but I certainly encourage everyone to adopt this trait as much as possible. I have met people who are content just going with the flow and watching their lives unfold before them. When I ask, they simply say that they don't have anything that they aspire to become or to accomplish.

Every person is different. I think it is a shame, though, not to have something to set your sights on and move toward. Just going through the planning and effort alone is a growing experience, even if the end goal has not yet been met or is in fact never met.

Often the fear of the unknown or the fear of failure is the unfortunate culprit that discourages setting lofty goals and striving to follow through with them. It is difficult to avoid allowing these fears to get in the way of your aspirations, but the key is to grit your teeth and do it anyway, even if the odds are that you will not succeed. As the old saying goes, the only way to ensure failure is not to make an attempt at all.

I am very thankful for the family that I was fortunate enough to grow up in and that shaped me into the person that I am today. To experience the family adventures that I was privileged to take part in throughout my childhood and adolescent years was a powerful growing and maturing opportunity, one that I hope that I can impart equally to my own children someday. Spending quality time as a family is such an important part of growing up, and unfortunately it is becoming less and less common among the families that I see nowadays.

The fact that we were a family undertaking the task together gave us some true advantages on the mountain, as well, that I think are worth mentioning. Firstly, it allowed us to effectively share tasks; each of us focusing the limited mental capacity we had at altitude on certain tasks while allowing the other members to focus on the remaining tasks.

This applied to making decisions as well. We could pool and consolidate our knowledge when it came to decision making, and although we did make some poor decisions along the way, we were able to come to educated conclusions most of the time by thinking and acting as a single unit whenever possible, in spite of the low-oxygen environment. Our objectives were aligned so that we had a unified goal that we were working together to achieve.

We also didn't feel hesitant or scared about putting our lives in each other's care, and we had a true interest in each other's success and safety, much more so, I believe, than is the case when climbers join with other climbers who are complete strangers at the beginning of the expedition. This gave us an added sense of security that someone was looking out for us, as well as an added degree of safety.

The trust that we had developed between each of us throughout our lives meant that we were that much more prepared to rely on each other and to act instinctively without hesitation when it was necessary to do so. In fact, often we were able to anticipate each other's actions and reactions to the challenges and harsh environment we were facing, which was a real benefit and helped us resolve conflicts and refocus that much more effectively.

Many people have asked us about the huge amount of preparation and training that must have been involved in order to ready ourselves for such a feat. The truth is that we did not do a lot of training at all, or at least nothing out of our ordinary. The major factor that prepared and readied us for what we had ahead of us was our choice of lifestyle and our passions.

Our entire lives, we have pursued adventure. Whether it was hiking in the Rocky Mountains or canoeing white water rivers, we were always staying active and picking up new skills for survival and success. Mallory vacations rarely involved going to the beach and relaxing; we were easily bored with those types of things, so we sought out adventure instead. So, in a way, our training was the lives we led.

There were so many unknowns on Everest and so many unexpected challenges that being prepared and equipped for the unknown was truly a necessity. And indeed, this is what our lifestyle choice prepared us for — taking head-on whatever the mountain threw at us.

There were things that truly amazed me about the human body and, in particular, my own body. As I explained at the beginning, I had started the climb with severe patellofemoral pain syndrome in both knees, and I could hardly walk up or down a small incline without very serious pain. Even with the aid of my patella support braces, it was difficult to move around even on flat ground.

Naturally, my spirits were down, and I was questioning whether or not I would even be able to make it to Base Camp. But surprisingly, and to my own astonishment, by gradually exposing my body to the tasks I needed it to accomplish, the pain slowly subsided. It was amazing to me how it all happened, because I was sure when I first developed the problem that what I needed was rest in order to recover; but that wasn't the case at all. I was able to completely remove the braces after a few days of trekking, and by the time I reached Base Camp, I felt almost no pain whatsoever.

The second amazing thing to me was the way the human body is able to condition itself for the extremely long days of climbing that we experienced, especially the long days around the time of our summit push. To climb for even a couple of hours up the steep terrain that we encountered would be difficult or impossible in our normal cardiovascular states, but by slowly pushing our bodies through further and more taxing tasks each day, they slowly adapted, and by the time we needed the energy and muscle conditioning to push ourselves upwards for twenty-plus hours straight, our bodies were able to perform.

Although my family's expedition on Everest was a fantastic experience, it is not one that I wish to go through again. For me, it was a once-in-a-lifetime adventure, an experience to learn and move on from. The worst times are soon forgotten, but the truth is that for a lot of the climb, we experienced sickness, harsh conditions, and sheer agony, both mentally and physically. I don't wish to go back and experience it over again, but I definitely don't regret taking on the experience in the first place.

Maybe my thirst for the high altitude will be rekindled in the coming years; only time will tell. There is definitely something about reaching the top of a high mountain that satisfies the needs within. I suppose it is human nature that makes us reach for higher places in life, and this is what I think fuels the desire for climbing. The sensation we get when we reach our goal is hard to put into words; it is something that you have to feel to fully understand.

I think perhaps renowned climber George Mallory explained this sensation or phenomenon best in his answer as to why he would attempt something as dangerous as climbing Mount Everest. His answer was plain and simple: "If you have to ask the question, you won't understand the answer."

George Mallory was a famous British mountaineer who made three attempts to summit Everest in the early 1920s, about thirty years before Edmund Hillary made his successful climb. On George's third attempt, in 1924, he and his climbing partner Sandy Irvine were last seen about 800 vertical feet from the summit; after that point, they disappeared and never returned.

George's body lay on the mountain, almost perfectly preserved by the frigid conditions, for nearly seventy-five years, until it was finally discovered by climbers in 1999.

There were clues discovered with George's body that suggest that George had actually made it to the summit of Everest and was on his way back down when he fell and ultimately lost his life.

First, he had carried a photograph of his wife that he was going to leave at the summit. When his body was discovered, the photograph was missing. He was also carrying snow goggles in his pocket, which would lead to the theory that he had made a push for the summit and was descending after sunset, when the goggles would no longer be required. Various oxygen cylinders were located, and the extent of oxygen usage supports the theory that he had reached the summit and was descending.

Whether George was indeed the first person to stand on the summit of Everest may never be verified, but his is an interesting story, and his accomplishments were incredible considering the very primitive clothing, equipment, and logistics that were available in those days.

As my family shares a common last name with George, we

are frequently asked if he is an ancestor of ours, and being curious ourselves, we did some digging into the question.

It turns out that my family is unusually connected with George, although there doesn't appear to be a direct blood link. We do, however, to the best of our knowledge share a common ancestor, Sir William Mallory. The story of the break in the bloodline is a bit confusing to the point that I'm not sure even I fully grasp it yet, but here it is:

Twelve generations back in our family tree, a Sir William Mallory (1525–1603) married Ursula Gale and had fifteen children. One of his sons, John, is the forebear of our side of the family tree, and another, Thomas, is forebear of the George Mallory side. Six generations below Thomas was born a man named John Holdsworth Mallory, born in Mobberley, Cheshire. John had two daughters but no son. One of the daughters, Julia, married a man called George Leigh.

George Leigh was given permission to marry Julia on one condition: that he add the word "Mallory" to his surname so that the Mallory name would not be lost when her father, John, passed away. Thus, George Leigh became George Leigh Mallory.

Julia died quite young, at the age of twenty-nine, and George remarried — a woman called Henrietta Trafford — and he felt no obligation to retain the "Mallory" surname, so he reverted back to George Leigh once again. That branch of the Mallory bloodline disappeared upon Julia's death.

George and Henrietta had a son called Herbert Leigh, who later in life decided to apply for a coat of arms — which is when the name Mallory popped up again. The church explained the history of his father having two different surnames in his two marriages, and the only way to rectify the problem was to re-christen himself Herbert Leigh Mallory.

Thus Herbert's eldest son, George Herbert Leigh, became George Herbert Leigh Mallory, the famous George Mallory who perished on Everest in 1924.

As a result of all this, there is an interesting connection between my family and George Mallory, and we are related through marriage, but as far as we know, he is not a direct blood relative.

32
Beyond Everest

IT WASN'T LONG BEFORE I WAS BACK INTO MY DAY-TO-DAY routine and the climb seemed almost like a distant memory. It seemed like a surreal escape from reality that we had been privy to for a time, a faraway adventure that brought a smile to my face whenever the recollection came to mind.

There were some true lessons that I learned from the expedition, though, and some knowledge that I will be able to take with me for the rest of my life.

I learned a fair bit about myself throughout the two-month expedition on the mountain. Going through the experience of nearly dying on the Summit Ridge definitely made me question a lot of things and think hard about what is truly important in life and what isn't. Sometimes it takes a drastic or traumatic event to trigger us into seeing the big picture more clearly. I was very close to losing my life on the mountain, and it helped me realize just how precious life is and how fragile it can be at times.

I would say one of the biggest things I learned was the need for patience — to resist rushing into things. The expedition was a true test of patience and dedicated perseverance. Lack of patience and perseverance is the major reason why so many climbers are unsuccessful at reaching the summit. We live in a society of instant gratification, and patiently waiting for something is often very difficult. It was difficult for me as well; I wanted to get the job done so I could move on. But only through patience and persistence can the summit be reached, and I had to learn this firsthand.

The second thing I learned was how to relax my mind and body and focus my energy on what was important. With the greatly decreased energy and mental capacity that we were left with at high altitude, this was essential. Overthinking things and second-guessing ourselves was not a luxury we had most of the time. We had to make a decision and execute that decision as efficiently as possible.

This energy conservation was also important when it came to letting the little things go. Stewing over disputes or disagreements was not an effective use of our time and energy, so the petty things had to be left behind.

Probably the most powerful thing that I learned about myself from our journey is that anything I really want in life and that I truly put my mind and effort into can be achieved. Our Everest summit definitely solidified this realization within me.

We have all heard this before, but I think it is a good thing to remind ourselves of, as we often seem to think it doesn't apply to us. It all depends on how badly we really want things to happen.

The truth is that if we set our minds on a specific path toward a particular goal and we nourish and build our willpower with positive and constructive thoughts along the way, there isn't anyone or anything in life that will be able to stop us. The power of the mind is an incredible force.

Life didn't stop for me or any of my family members after the climb, and we all moved on fairly quickly to our next ambitions.

My father finished his goal of climbing the Seven Summits and became the first person to accomplish this feat along with at least one other member of his family on each ascent. In December of 2010, he reached the top of the final peak of the Seven Summits: the Vinson Massif, the highest mountain in Antarctica.

Adam and Laura climbed alongside him and reached the top as well, but I decided to opt out of that particular climb, as I had just recently married and I didn't think it would be fair to leave Natalie and embark on another risky endeavour so shortly afterwards. I suppose my priorities have changed a little now, although I will never lose the adventuresome spirit. I will always continue to seek out new challenges, as I am sure the rest of my family will as well.

Adam and Laura intend to follow in Dad's footsteps and climb all of the Seven Summits. At the time of this writing, Adam has completed four of the seven, and Laura has completed six. I have no doubt that they will both achieve this feat in the coming years. As for myself, I don't think that I have the same desire. Although it is something I may revisit later in life, at this point my priorities and goals don't involve any more high-altitude adventures. There are so many other things that I want to do and accomplish in life that my slate is getting very full.

It was the summer of 2010 when Natalie and I were married, and we wanted to begin our marriage with a unique adventure, so one week after our honeymoon, we packed our bags and moved to Santiago, Chile, in South America, where we lived and worked for almost two years. I worked as a mechanical engineer on various copper-related projects, and Natalie was able to work in the translations department, improving the quality of any English documents that had been translated to send out to clients.

It was an incredible experience and a bold move that I would recommend to any newlywed couple, as it forced us to be reliant on each other and quickly develop our independence from family and friends. After Chile, we moved to Arizona, where we lived for two years before making our way back home to Canada. The next generation of Mallorys arrived in the summer of 2013 when Natalie and I welcomed our daughter into the world, Aria Danielle Mallory. Our son, Oaklan Wib Mallory, arrived in the winter of 2016. They will soon find out the adventures that are in store for them, growing up as Mallorys!

Since Everest, my focus has been more on internal or psychological advancement rather than purely on the types of physical or external challenges that we encountered on the mountain. I have taken a keen interest in what makes people truly happy in life and how I can diminish or ideally eliminate mental stresses and unhappiness from my own life.

The more I delve into it, the more I discover just how complicated our minds really are, but I believe it is possible to be completely happy and content no matter what our daily tasks are or what difficult or taxing situations we find ourselves facing. It all comes down to how we react and interpret the experiences and situations we find ourselves in on a day-to-day basis.

Although I consider myself to be a fairly social and confident person, I have struggled with high anxiety in certain social or pressure situations at different times in my life, and it has been a real challenge to push through and overcome. I think part of the problem is that I am so analytical that I get stuck in my mind trying to resolve matters. I get caught up in cycles of continuous thought, trying to figure things out, which is sometimes impossible and even detrimental on the emotional level, because the continuous figuring in itself usually is contributing to the pain or anxiety I am trying to avoid. Of course, this becomes a self-fulfilling prophecy, and it can be a difficult cycle to break free of.

I am thankful for the emotional challenges I have, though, as they force me to continue to learn and develop myself. There is nothing worse than hearing about the people who simply give up and resort to substance abuse or self-harm because they cannot cope with their lives.

As time progresses, I am continuing to understand more and more the challenges of the mind, partly because of the struggles I have had in my own life and partly because I have become much more open to information and ideas, no matter how abstract they seem. There are some strange theories and claims about the human psyche out there, but I don't discount anything anymore until I have given it a fair assessment or put it to the test.

I look at people's fears from a different perspective now. I don't excuse or tolerate unreasonable fear in myself or others, but I do better understand the struggles that people go through and how difficult it can be to overcome these phobias, especially if they are purely psychological.

I have made a lot of progress in my study and mastery of thoughts and emotions, although I still have a long way to go.

Although this book is built primarily around my family's expedition on Everest, what I hope you take away from this book is much more than just inspiration from our journey on the mountain. The underlying message I have tried to portray is about our journey as a family and the choices and lifestyles that have made our family into what most people would consider a success. We do have our difficulties and disagreements at times, but to continue to connect and truly enjoy spending time together is a rare and special circumstance that is not all that common.

I really have my parents to thank for this, as I am mostly just the recipient. But I think the techniques and conditions that my parents raised us in are similar to those that I would like to replicate for the family that Natalie and I are now nurturing and growing.

What I believe contributes most to the success of a family is the simple act of making time to do things together and doing them on a regular basis — finding things that are enjoyable to everyone so that spending time together is more of a privilege than a task.

My parents didn't do everything right; no parents do. But spending quality time with your children is an important choice, and I believe it pays dividends in the end. I know a few very successful people with plenty of money but a broken family and nobody, really, to share it with. The result is endless questioning of past decisions and a life full of regret.

I hope that I will be able to raise my own children well and instil in them the passion for living life to its absolute fullest.

One of my new, rewarding challenges that I began undertaking shortly after our climb is inspirational speaking and training, based not only on my family's expedition on Everest, but on other subjects that I have been studying for myself relating to continuous improvement of individuals and teams. I have become something of an expert in the fields of leadership and human performance, and I really enjoy sharing my knowledge and expertise in these areas.

I continued working as an engineer and project manager for almost eight years after the climb but eventually I realized that if I didn't pursue my own ambitions and develop my own business, I would always look back and think, "what if?" I didn't want to go through life always wondering about a missed opportunity so, in 2015, I made the decision to focus my efforts more fully on speaking, training and consulting in the areas I am most passionate about. I have been thoroughly enjoying this new venture and the unique opportunities and challenges that it has presented me.

It has been a fantastic learning experience and beneficial for me as well in my journey of continuous improvement. Standing in front of groups of people and delivering my messages makes me feel alive and allows me to connect with others on a whole new level. I get a lot of enjoyment from inspiring people to accomplish their dreams as well, and it gives me great satisfaction to receive the many comments and feedback on the inspiration my sessions and my family's story have been to so many people.

I hope that throughout this book and the sharing of my family's journey on Mount Everest, I have also been able to convey some of the underlying traits that contributed not only to our success as a team on the mountain but also to our success in general as a close-knit and committed family. None of us gets the opportunity to choose the family we are born into, but there are always ways to improve and deepen the interactions we have with our family members.

There were several different elements that were important during our expedition, and many of them I have touched on throughout the pages of this book, but I believe there were three principal traits in particular that were of paramount importance to our safety and success. Many other elements were important as well, but most of these can be classified under or form part of these three principal traits.

These same qualities that helped to improve and strengthen our family dynamics are, of course, equally as important and relevant to interactions we have with friends, co-workers, and others we associate with throughout our daily activities.

The first element — which I touched on earlier but is worth repeating because it was probably the most important factor in our success — is developing and maintaining a strong level of trust. Trust is essential for healthy and effective team dynamics as well as building lasting relationships. Without trust, teams fall apart, relationships fail, and families become broken.

Of course, there is more to the development of trust than simply deciding that trust is important and committing to uphold it. Often it takes both a significant amount of time and many positive reference experiences for a sufficient level of trust to be reached. We were fortunate enough to have been given the opportunity to develop this level of trust through the many other excursions we had taken part in together.

Underneath the broad heading of trust are many related traits that contribute to its development and as a general rule go hand-in-hand. These include such traits as respect, commitment, reliance on one another, and a willingness to make concessions, and a healthy and open approach to communication. Each of these is a conscious choice that we have to make and continue to commit to. It takes both effort and discipline to develop and maintain these traits, but they are keys to the development of trust.

The second element that was essential to our success is willpower. Having the ability and determination to control oneself and to manage the automatic emotional responses that often take over and drive us off course was paramount. This is not usually a comfortable thing to do as it requires a degree of self-discipline and often involves breaking away from typical thought patterns that have become second nature.

Each of us is different and truly knowing yourself and understanding what drives your decisions is a key ingredient in developing willpower. The life path we ultimately take really comes down to what we allow ourselves to focus on. Without conscious effort it is easy for our focus to be swayed by external stimuli as our minds jump chaotically from one idea to another, but this rarely results in progress towards what we really want in life. It is through consciously controlling our focus that we stay on course.

Willpower was also important when it came to having effective methods of dealing with and overcoming conflicts that arose, both internally and externally.

On the individual level, there was often almost a steady stream of internal struggles going on. The temptation to turn back is the most obvious, and it is a powerful force indeed, because the vast majority of climbers do succumb to the temptation and give up before the end of the two-month journey, no matter how much time, money, and energy they have invested.

After being there, I can certainly attest to the psychological tug-of-war that all climbers go through. It takes a certain type of mental fortitude to keep putting one foot in front of the other in spite of the constant desire to yield and return to what is comfortable and familiar. This type of mental toughness can be developed, systematically, one challenge at a time, by studying yourself and how your mind works and reacts to different situations. By consistently making the decision to carry on when the temptation to quit asserts itself, this mental strength is progressively being developed and reinforced.

In addition to the struggle over whether or not to continue, there are many other internal dilemmas to deal with, many of them centred on things like resolving the horrible sicknesses and biological adaptations the body is going through, avoiding destructive thinking patterns, and dealing with the boredom and isolation that the acclimatization process generates. Each of these internal struggles is in itself very demanding and problematic, but the cumulative effect of having to deal with them all simultaneously makes them nearly insurmountable.

There are also many external conflicts that arise from spending prolonged periods of time with other climbers. Attitudes and egos take over, and being exposed at the same time to miserable living conditions only intensifies the problem. This puts climbers in a heightened state of irritability and often leads to serious arguments and heated disputes. There are even occasions when physical violence has broken out between climbers who have allowed their tempers to build to the point of losing control.

Having a method or effective approach to dealing with these conflicts is vital. It is a difficult thing to do, but maintaining your resolve and seeing the conflict from a higher level without letting your emotional reactions take over can help prevent situations from escalating. On the mountain, we were able to avoid most of the quarrels that took place at Base Camp with other climbers by simply not allowing ourselves to be drawn in.

It again comes down mostly to a matter of focus. Whether we absorb destructive comments and situations into our psyche and allow them to become the centre of our focus or we choose to dwell on more important issues is what ultimately determines how affected and involved we will become.

We did have some minor disagreements throughout the expedition, not only with other climbers but also within our family and between our Sherpas and ourselves, but we worked through them as quickly as we could and didn't allow our primary focus to be derailed.

The third essential quality my family and I have developed over the years, which has truly benefited us in all areas and certainly was key to our success on the mountain, is resilience. Being able to bounce back and readily regain control and balance after being knocked off course by the unexpected challenges that presented themselves time and time again on the expedition was essential. No matter how much preparation and research we did to anticipate what the mountain had in store for us, almost on a daily basis there were new, unique challenges to deal with.

An essential part of being resilient is also persevering and pushing on through the challenges as you adapt and accept each of them. It starts with making up your mind, at the deepest level, that you will continue on no matter what roadblocks appear along the way.

Fortunately, resilience is something that can be developed and increased. Preparing ourselves both mentally and physically for the unknown as much as possible can increase our resilience in most situations. As well, resilience can be developed by slowly exposing ourselves to greater and greater challenges, overcoming them one by one. Each challenge that we are able to navigate through and recuperate from builds our resilience one step at a time. It is often an uncomfortable thing to do, but venturing beyond our comfort zones and always tackling a little more than we are accustomed to taking on definitely helps to build this resilience.

Trust, willpower, and resilience are qualities that we as human beings already possess to some degree, but in our continuous journey of self-discovery, we can always benefit from a better understanding and improvement in each of these areas. My family is fortunate to have had so many opportunities to practise and develop each of these. In essence, we have acted as coaches to each other, whether intentionally or not, through the many different adventures we have been involved in together, and in the end I believe this was the major factor in our success on the mountain.

It is a matter of choice whether or not each of us further develops these qualities within ourselves, but if we pursue continuous improvement in these areas, we can achieve success in all aspects of life, including our lifelong dreams.

To conclude this book, I think it is fitting for me to sum everything up with a favourite quote of mine from Sir Edmund Hillary himself. These are wonderful words that I think apply not only to climbing but to the vast majority of challenges we face throughout our journey here on earth.

When asked about how he felt after conquering Mount Everest, Hillary responded: "It's not the mountain we conquer but ourselves."

Looking back on our journey on Mount Everest, I think these words could not ring more true. The most difficult part of the climb, or any other major accomplishment, is almost always the mental challenge of facing our fears and overcoming our own reservations and limitations. If we can do this, we can do anything.

About the Author

ALAN MALLORY IS AN INTERNATIONAL SPEAKER, AUTHOR and professional development coach who is passionate about leadership and living life to the absolute fullest! He studied engineering at Queen's University and has worked all over the world as a mechanical engineer and project manager but his true passion is in working with people to reach new heights in the way we think and the actions we take. Alan has always had a keen interest in discovering what drives us to do what we do and how we can use this knowledge to improve our lives and the lives of those around us. In his free time, Alan loves to travel and explore new places with his family and friends. He is an avid adventurer and enjoys many different activities although his favourites are those spent out in the wilderness and those that involve strategy and problem solving. As a prominent speaker at conferences and conventions, Alan delivers a number of exciting presentations and training programs that are all about embracing and working through challenges as well as exploring the skills and mindsets that allow great leaders and committed teams to achieve breakthrough performance. By integrating his years of innovative leadership experience with captivating mountaineering and adventure stories, Alan creates a powerful and unforgettable journey for his audience.

For more information,
please visit www.AlanMallory.com